AMERICAN FOREIGN POLICY

opposing viewpoints

AMERICAN FOREIGN POLICY

opposing viewpoints

David L. Bender

OPPOSING VIEWPOINTS SERIES

SECOND EDITION

Greenhaven Press

**577 SHOREVIEW PARK ROAD
ST. PAUL, MINNESOTA 55112**

Second Edition
Revised and Enlarged

© Copyright 1972, 1981 by Greenhaven Press, Inc.

ISBN 0-89908-311-0 Paper Edition
ISBN 0-89908-336-6 Library Edition

CONGRESS SHALL MAKE NO LAW... ABRIDGING THE FREEDOM OF SPEECH, OR OF THE PRESS

first amendment to the U.S. Constitution

The basic foundation of our democracy is the first amendment guarantee of freedom of expression. The OPPOSING VIEW-POINTS SERIES is dedicated to the concept of this basic freedom and the idea that it is more important to practice it than to enshrine it.

TABLE OF CONTENTS

Page

the Opposing viewpoints series

THE IMPORTANCE OF EXAMINING OPPOSING VIEWPOINTS

The purpose of this book, and the Opposing Viewpoints Series as a whole, is to confront you with alternative points of view on complex and sensitive issues.

Perhaps the best way to inform yourself is to analyze the positions of those who are regarded as experts and well studied on the issues. It is important to consider every variety of opinion in an attempt to determine the truth. Opinions from the mainstream of society should be examined. Also important are opinions that are considered radical, reactionary, minority or stigmatized by some other uncomplimentary label. An important lesson of history is the fact that many unpopular and even despised opinions eventually gained widespread acceptance. The opinions of Socrates, Jesus and Galileo are good examples of this.

You will approach this book with opinions of your own on the issues debated within it. To have a good grasp of your own viewpoint you must understand the arguments of those with whom you disagree. It is said that those who do not completely understand their adversary's point of view do not fully understand their own.

Perhaps the most persuasive case for considering opposing viewpoints has been presented by John Stuart Mill in his work *On Liberty*. Consider the following statements of his when studying controversial issues.

THE OPINIONS OF OTHERS

If all mankind minus one were of one opinion, and only one person were of the contrary opinion, mankind would be no more justified in silencing that one person than he, if he had the power, would be justified in silencing mankind....

We can never be sure that the opinion we are endeavoring to stifle is a false opinion...

All silencing of discussion is an assumption of infallibility....

Ages are no more infallible than individuals; every age having held many opinions which subsequent ages have deemed not only false but absurd; and it is as certain that many opinions now general will be rejected by future ages....

The only way in which a human being can make some approach to knowing the whole of a subject, is by hearing what can be said about it by persons of every variety of opinion, and studying all modes in which it can be looked at by every character of mind. No wise man ever acquired his wisdom in any mode but this....

The beliefs which we have most warrant for have no safeguard to rest on but a standing invitation to the whole world to prove them unfounded....

To call any proposition certain, while there is any one who would deny its certainty if permitted, but who is not permitted, is to assume that we ourselves and those who agree with us are the judges of certainty, and judges without hearing the other side....

Men are not more zealous for truth than they are for error, and a sufficient application of legal or even social penalties will generally succeed in stopping the propagation of either....

However unwilling a person who has a strong opinion may admit the possibility that his opinion may be false, he ought to be moved by the consideration that, however true it may be, if it is not fully, frequently, and fearlessly discussed, it will be a dead dogma, not a living truth.

From *On Liberty* by John Stuart Mill.

A pitfall to avoid in considering alternative points of view is that of regarding your own point of view as being merely common sense and the most rational stance, and the point of view of others as being only opinion and naturally wrong. It may be that the opinion of others is correct and that yours is in error.

Another pitfall to avoid is that of closing your mind to the opinions of those whose views differ from yours. The best way to approach a dialogue is to make your primary purpose that of understanding the mind and arguments of the other person and not that of enlightening him or her with your solutions. One learns more by listening than by speaking.

It is my hope that after reading this book you will have a deeper understanding of the issues debated and will appreciate the complexity of even seemingly simple issues when good and honest people disagree. This awareness is particularly important in a democratic society such as ours, where people enter into public debate to determine the common good. People with whom you disagree should not be regarded as enemies, but rather as friends who suggest a different path to a common goal.

ANALYZING SOURCES OF INFORMATION

The Opposing Viewpoints Series uses diverse sources; magazines, journals, books, newspapers, statements and position papers from a wide range of individuals and organizations. These sources help in the development of a mindset that is open to the consideration of a variety of opinions.

The format of the Opposing Viewpoints Series should help you answer the following questions.

1. *Are you aware that three of the most popular weekly news magazines, Time, Newsweek, and U.S. News and World Report are not totally objective accounts of the news?*
2. **Do you know there is no such thing as a completely objective author, book, newspaper or magazine?**
3. **Do you think that because a magazine or newspaper article is unsigned it is always a statement of facts rather than opinions?**
4. **How can you determine the point of view of newspapers and magazines?**
5. **When you read do you question an author's frame of reference (political persuasion, training, and life experience)?**

Many people finish their formal education unable to cope with these basic questions. They have little chance to understand the social forces and issues surrounding them. Some fall easy victims to demagogues preaching solutions to problems by scapegoating minorities with conspiratorial and paranoid explanations of complex social issues.

I do not want to imply that anything is wrong with authors and publications that have a political slant or bias. All authors have a frame of reference. Readers should understand this. You should also understand that almost all writers have a point of view. An important skill in reading is to be able to locate and identify a point of view. This series gives you practice in both.

DEVELOPING BASIC THINKING SKILLS

A number of basic skills for critical thinking are practiced in the discussion activities that appear throughout the books in the series. Some of the skills are:

Locating a Point of View The ability to determine which side of an issue an author supports.

Evaluating Sources of Information The ability to choose from among alternative sources the most reliable and accurate source in relation to a given subject.

Distinguishing Between Primary and Secondary Sources The ability to understand the important distinction between sources which are primary (original or eyewitness accounts) and those which are secondary (historically removed from, and based on, primary sources).

Separating Fact from Opinion The ability to make the basic distinction between factual statements (those which can be demonstrated or verified empirically) and statements of opinion (those which are beliefs or attitudes that cannot be proved).

Distinguishing Between Prejudice and Reason The ability to differentiate between statements of prejudice (unfavorable, preconceived judgments based on feelings instead of reason) and statements of reason (conclusions that can be clearly and logically explained or justified).

Identifying Stereotypes The ability to identify oversimplified, exaggerated descriptions (favorable or unfavorable) about people and insulting statements about racial, religious or national groups, based upon misinformation or lack of information.

Recognizing Ethnocentrism The ability to recognize attitudes or opinions that express the view that one's own race, culture, or group is inherently superior, or those attitudes that judge another race, culture, or group in terms of one's own.

It is important to consider opposing viewpoints. It is equally important to be able to critically analyze those viewpoints. The discussion activities in this book will give you practice in mastering these thinking skills.

Using this book, and others in the series, will help you develop critical thinking skills. These skills should improve your ability to better understand what you read. You should be better able to separate fact from opinion, reason from rhetoric. You should become a better consumer of information in our media-centered culture.

A VALUES ORIENTATION

Throughout the Opposing Viewpoints Series you are presented conflicting values. A good example is *American Foreign Policy*. The first chapter debates whether foreign policy should be based on the same kind of moral principles that individuals use in guiding their personal actions, or instead be based primarily on doing what best advances national interests, regardless of moral implications.

The series does not advocate a particular set of values. Quite the contrary! The very nature of the series leaves it to you, the reader, to formulate the values orientation that you find most suitable. My purpose, as editor of the series, is to see that this is made possible by offering a wide range of viewpoints which are fairly presented.

David L. Bender
Opposing Viewpoints Series Editor

Chapter

AMERICAN FOREIGN POLICY

What Are the Goals of American Foreign Policy?

"We must take the lead in pointing out to other nations, and particularly those of the Third World, the superiority of our system."

A Foreign Policy for a Proud America

Ronald Reagan

President Ronald Reagan has been criticized for not making a general statement on the foreign policy of his administration. The following viewpoint is excerpted from a speech he made to the Chicago Council of Foreign Relations on March 17, 1980. It presents a good overview of what appears to be his approach to foreign policy. To keep abreast of developments in his administration's policy, consult the *Department of State Bulletin* which most libraries carry and which is published monthly.

Consider the following questions while reading:
1. What "three broad requirements" does President Reagan suggest for American foreign policy?
2. Why does Mr. Reagan claim "we are losing out in global economic competition"?
3. What "grand strategy" does the president recommend?

Ronald Reagan, "A Foreign Policy For a Proud America," *Human Events*, April 5, 1980. Reprinted with permission from *Human Events*.

We now face a situation in which our principal adversary, the Soviet Union, surpasses us in virtually every category of military strength.

While the Soviets arrogantly warn us to stay out of their way, we occupy ourselves by looking for human rights violations in those countries which have historically been our friends and allies. Those friends feel betrayed and abandoned, and in several specific cases they have been.

A Soviet satellite state operates freely just 90 miles off our coast; our embassies are targets for terrorist attacks; our diplomats have been murdered...

We all have been dishonored, and our credibility as a great nation compromised, to say the least. Our shield has been tarnished.

We are a proud nation, with much in our history of which to be rightfully proud...

All over America I have found the people hungry to be told the truth about our situation and ready to respond in the country's hour of need. The American people are not ready to consign the American dream, with all that it means to us and to oppressed people everywhere to the dustbin of history.

THE PATH WE MUST TAKE

May I suggest an alternate path this nation can take; a change in foreign policy from the vacillation, appeasement and aimlessness of our present policy?

That alternate path must meet three broad requirements.

First, it must be based on firm convictions, inspired by a clear vision of, and belief in, America's future.

Second, it calls for a strong economy, based on the free market system, which gave us an unchallenged leadership in creative technology.

Third, and very simply, we must have the unquestioned capability to preserve world peace and our national security.

When I say our foreign policy must be based on convictions, I speak of our belief in the principles and ideals which made this nation what it is today. We must take the lead in

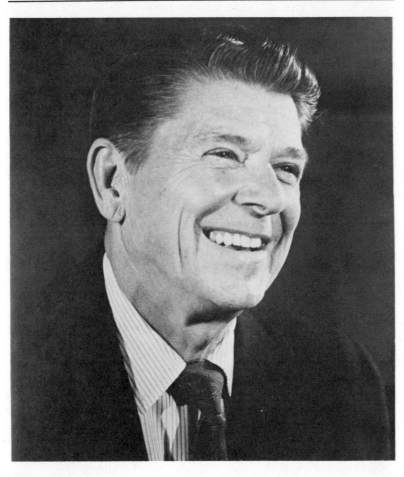

Ronald Reagan

pointing out to other nations, and particularly those of the Third World, the superiority of our system. For too long at official levels we have been apologetic about, if not downright hostile toward, American capitalism as a model for economic development.

We must also use our ability to communicate with the world —through the Voice of America, Radio Free Europe and Radio Liberty—to call attention to those nations that also were once poor but now enjoy a standard of living far above that of their neighbors who put their faith in communism. We can, for example, point to a Singapore, a Taiwan or a South Korea, as nations that shunned Marxism and socialism and have won their prosperity by means of private enterprise, thrift and hard work.

Coming to the second of our broad requirements, we cannot meet our world responsibilities without a strong economic policy which is effective at home and in the world marketplace. We cannot go on allowing government to spend beyond its means while our currency depreciates in value literally by the day and week...

We are losing out in global economic competition not only because we have become overgoverned, over-regulated and overtaxed, but because our method of taxation has discouraged investment, risk and enterprise, and the result of over-taxation has frightened people from the private sector, which accounts for our production, to the public sector, which is not only the least productive segment of our economy, but actually devotes much of its activity to impeding production and stimulating consumption. Today only about 79 million Americans work and earn in the productive private sector. About 82 million get a portion of their income from government.

An unbalanced administration of the antitrust laws has led to compulsory licensing of new technologies that benefits foreign competitors. Our foreign competitors are free to pool their resources so as to drive American business out of foreign markets. Our antitrust policies—designed to foster competition in the American market—are applied to American firms in the world market in such a way as to make them noncompetitive with other industrialized nations.

We must put our economic house in order so we can once again show the world by example that ours is the best system for all who want security and freedom.

Communism is good for guaranteeing lifetime jobs for dictators, but it is terrible for economic development. This is a fact that we have to get across to the people throughout the world, and especially in the poorer countries. The American success story used to be a shining example, something that other people aspired to. It was and can still be the American dream. But the world must see that we still believe in that dream.

And this brings us to the third requirement for our policy.

18

The best foreign policy cannot preserve the peace and protect the realm of freedom unless it is backed up by adequate military power...

To rebuild our military strength will take determination, prudence, and a sustained effort. We simply have to face the harsh fact that our defense posture must be invigorated across the board.

To prevent the ultimate catastrophe of a massive nuclear attack, we urgently need a program to preserve and restore our strategic deterrent...

THE TRUMAN DOCTRINE

It must be the policy of the United States to support free peoples who are resisting attempted subjugation by armed minorities or by outside pressure...The free peoples of the world look to us for support in maintaining their freedoms. If we falter in our leadership, we may endanger the peace of the world — and we shall surely endanger the welfare of this nation.

Harry S. Truman (1947)

We have to maintain a superior navy. We are a nation with vital interests and commitments overseas, and our navy must stay ahead of the Soviet buildup. This means commissioning the ships and developing technology which will enable the United States to command the oceans for decades to come.

We must restore an active ready reserve force and provide the necessary incentives to retain skilled men and women in the armed forces. I believe we can make a voluntary force work. But we can't when we force people to serve at a pay scale lower than welfare. A noncommissioned officer on a carrier is put in charge of a $25-million aircraft. He often works 16 hours a day. He earns less than a cashier at a supermarket. Is it any wonder the armed forces are losing two-thirds of their personnel?...

We have to take full advantage of the contributions that American science and technology can make to the defense of the United States and to the preservation of peace.

And we must once again restore the United States intelligence community. A Democratic Congress, aided and abetted by the Carter Administration, has succeeded in shackling and demoralizing our intelligence services to the point that they no longer function effectively as a component part of our defenses. With all of the terrorist and military threats confronting us, we need a first-class intelligence capability, with high morale and dedicated people. We have the means to regenerate our intelligence organization, and I would surely employ those means.

But while we do all these things and they are essential, we must above all have a grand strategy; a plan for the dangerous decade ahead. We must be prepared with contingency plans for future Irans and Afghanistans. It is painfully apparent that we have been surprised repeatedly and faced with situations we have never anticipated and for which we have no ready plan of action...

Totalitarian Marxists are in control of the Caribbean island of Grenada, where Cuban advisers are now training guerrillas for subversive action against other countries such as Trinidad – Tobago, Grenada's democratic neighbor. In El Salvador, Marxist totalitarian revolutionaries, supported by Havana and Moscow, are preventing the construction of a democratic government.

Must we let Grenada, Nicaragua, El Salvador, all become additional "Cubas," new outposts for Soviet combat brigades? Will the next push of the Moscow–Havana axis be northward to Guatemala and thence to Mexico, and south to Costa Rica and Panama?

In the United Nations — where we pay the lion's share of a bloated budget — Puerto Rico and Guam are alleged to be instances of colonialism, yet hardly a single speech is being given, hardly a word is said about the vast expanse of the colonial empire of the Soviet Union...

OUR GRAND STRATEGY

Our grand strategy must recognize those areas of the world which are necessary to any plan for preserving world peace.

Here in our own hemisphere I urge a North American Accord to bind the three great nations of this continent closer together. I have already spoken of Central America and of the Caribbean, and certainly we must regain the friendship and trust of the nations of South America.

In the Middle East our alignment with Israel must be continued for the benefit of both countries. Israel, a stable democracy sharing our own values, serves as a vital strategic asset with its highly trained and experienced military forces, and is a deterrent to Soviet expansion in that troubled part of the world.

We must continue efforts to win the friendship and trust of

the other nations of the Middle East, but we must not attempt to impose our solution to the problems there. This can be said of the trouble in Lebanon, where we should offer our help but without dictating terms, and it also applies to the tragedy involving two of our NATO allies over Cyprus.

We did not seek leadership of the free world, but there is no one else who can provide it. And without our leadership there will be no peace in the world.

Finally, we must rid ourselves of the "Vietnam Syndrome." It has dominated our thinking for too long.

The conduct of American foreign policy is essentially a task of effectively managing our resources—material, human and moral—and implementing policies which utilize those resources in the pursuit of our national interests...

I have long felt that our foreign policy must be changed, and I have consistently stressed the urgency of strengthening our defenses against Russia's growing military might. I have made a strenuous effort to alert my fellow Americans that the policy of detente is, to a large extent, an illusion and not a reality of East–West relations...

Today, even though our nation's security has greatly deteriorated during these past years, my confidence in the strength and patriotism of the American people remains unshaken.

If told the truth, the American people will support a foreign policy reflecting their pride and patriotism, a foreign policy that is a charter for our nation's great future, not an installment plan for America's decline.

When our national recovery begins, you will see a rallying of the spirit not only in this great nation, but among all oppressed people, and a revival of our alliances throughout the world.

Once we act again as the leader of the Free World, I believe we will no longer stand alone; we will be supported by a grand coalition of other nations and peoples who want to work with us to preserve their freedom.

We have the resources, we have the wisdom, and we have the conviction to preserve peace and security in the coming decade. We have only to get on with the tasks before us.

"For the past decade the American people have had neither collective discipline nor a sense of national honor... As long as that situation endures, they will have no peace."

Why American Foreign Policy Does Not Work

Bernard E. Brown

Bernard E. Brown is a professor of Political Science at City University of New York. He earned both his MA and PhD degrees from Columbia University. A frequent contributor to many professional journals, Dr. Brown is the author of *The American Political System* (1967). In the following viewpoint, he claims that the changes forced upon the government following the Vietnam War and the Watergate incident have weakened the executive branch to the point where the president is rendered incapable of providing firm leadership.

Consider the following questions while reading:

1. **The author claims American foreign policy is ineffective because of "The Vietnam Syndrome" and "The Watergate Syndrome". What are they? How have they crippled our foreign policy?**
2. **What is needed, in the author's opinion, to revitalize American foreign policy?**

Reprinted with permission from the April, 1980 issue of *Newsletter* published by the National Committee On American Foreign Policy.

In the course of the 1970s, there came into being a "Vietnam–Watergate syndrome" far more important than the "China Syndrome" starring the irrepressible Jane Fonda. A sudden sagging of American leadership has been the inevitable result of the Vietnam–Watergate syndrome...

THE VIETNAM SYNDROME

The Vietnam War was a straight fight between two authoritarian groups or coalitions for control of a society breaking out of its traditional and colonial mold. Few such societies are ready for civil liberties and parliamentary democracy because the necessary social and economic conditions are lacking. One authoritarianism was embodied by the Vietnamese Communist party, which received massive military aid from the Soviet Union and China. It departed in no significant way from the Leninist–Stalinist model: sacred texts, a glorious leader, the principle of democratic centralism guaranteeing mass enthusiasm in carrying out decisions made by a self-selected leadership, purges, the repression of dissent, the aspiration toward totalitarian control of the society, the promise of reform as a tactic in the seizure of power, and so on. The other authoritarianism was a milder version found frequently in the third world, in which a small Western-oriented native elite seeks to forward development or modernization through a variety of contradictory policies—paternalism, liberalism, nascent capitalism, state socialism, planning, technical assistance, and so on. Despite all its drawbacks, the Western-inspired model offers a far greater range of opportunities for dissent, criticism, and even for material progress than does its communist rival. Communist regimes are notoriously inept at creating high standards of living for their people. But this is a minor point. Occasionally people need firm direction more than increased wealth...

What a contrast is the Vietnam syndrome! The communists were proclaimed not only the wave of the future but historically correct. They were a "fire in the lake," burning out the corruption of bourgeois morality and traditionalism through the intensity of their revolutionary passion...

The next step was to identify the United States as the mainstay and then the source of evil in the world, as revealed through Hegelian and Marxist concepts that somehow justified bureaucratic terror and Asian Gulags. For some the devil in America was capitalism; for others it was modernity itself. But in practice it did not matter. Whatever weakened the West and the United States in particular must favor the revolutionary cause and hence was "true" in a transcendental Hegelian sense.

FROM VIETNAM TO IRAN

The Vietnam syndrome has permeated the American political class. The evidence: American policy in the Iranian crisis. When militants seized control of the embassy and took hostages, the reaction — as in the good old days of student protest—was to recognize the legitimacy of the self-appointed spokesmen of the revolution and enter into negotiations. The Iranian militants bound and blindfolded American diplomats, playfully poking them with rifles as they paraded them around for the delectation of the world press. Here was a reenactment of that celebrated photograph showing the last American helicopter leaving Saigon—a picture worth a dozen divisions of paratroops. Why object? Did not a large number of American intellectuals and politicians flock to the Beacon Theater in New York to thank the Vietnamese communists for the occupation of Saigon and conquest of all Vietnam? No criticism of Vietnamese communists is ever to be uttered, not even when they expel the Chinese community, create a repressive regime in the south, or invade Cambodia. Similarly, it may never be mentioned that the Ayatollah Khomeiny represents a fundamentalist reaction to science and rationality in a traditional society. The magic word REVOLUTION is a cleansing wind that blows away all doubts.

STRENGTHENING FOREIGN POLICY

There is no sure way to protect foreign policy from meddling and obstructionism by congressional cliques. U.S. diplomacy, however, would almost automatically become more consistent, credible and effective if Congress, at its own initiative, demonstrated discipline and bipartisanship in offering advice and consent to the Executive Branch...

Strobe Talbott, *Time*, February 23, 1981.

It is hardly surprising that the American political class was unable to cope with the propaganda of Khomeiny and the militants because all "revolutionary" assertions were deemed valid beforehand. Thus the United States is the "devil", American blacks are oppressed and should rise up in revolt; the CIA is responsible for all mischief in the world, including the shah's secret police; the third world has been looted by the West and especially by the United States; and so on. Who will reply that most American blacks have a standard of living approximately equal to that of European whites (not to mention the poverty-stricken victims of reactionary theology in Iran); that the CIA is a boy-scout troop compared to the KGB or Cuban intelligence and, in any event, not much different from British or French intelligence agencies; that third-world police need no outside technical assistance in order to behave with brutality—as the Iranian "revolutionary guards" are now demonstrating; and that the poverty of preindustrial societies is a function of their own immobility rather than Western exploitation.

The response of the American government to the seizure of its embassy in Teheran was characteristic; to assemble experts, put all relevant data through computers, and assume that somehow, a policy would materialize. The computers clicked away like mad; but in the absence of political vision, no policy was or could be forthcoming. That, too, is part of the Vietnam syndrome: Turn policy over to "experts," computers, and lawyers. Why were not Iranian diplomats in the United States immediately interned and held for future exchange? Such a decision was beyond the ken of those who program computers and beyond the competence of lawyers. In the wake of Vietnam and Watergate, political vision has been replaced by a rampant legalism.

FROM IRAN TO AFGHANISTAN

The crisis in Afghanistan is another spin-off of Vietnam and its syndrome. Why did the Russians invade and occupy Afghanistan? For a simple reason: They knew perfectly well that no force in the world could stop them or compel them to withdraw once the occupation was accomplished. Two years ago the Russians stage-managed a coup d'etat in Kabul, and there was no American or Western reaction whatsoever. The Russians were entitled to assume that no one cares...

The Russians, then, had every reason to believe that they could act in Afghanistan with impunity. Olympic boycotts and economic sanctions are merely annoyances, and they cut two ways. Above all, the Russians fear a firm American declaration that the communist regime in Afghanistan is repressive, that the Afghan people are justified in their revolt, and that it is only natural that they will find the arms they require for victorious resistance. But such a declaration—backed up by action—is beyond the capacity or the imagination of the American political class today.

THE WATERGATE SYNDROME

That "great beast" (as Alexander Hamilton is alleged once to have said), the American people, is beginning to stir. The combination of humiliation and helplessness is provoking irritation and discontent. But the pendulum will *not* swing back soon toward an affirmative foreign policy. On top of the Vietnam syndrome, which brought about the present crisis, is the Watergate syndrome, which makes it impossible to resolve the crisis.

Watergate was a political calamity...

Political passions in 1972 were so inflamed that partisanship was carried beyond the point of democratic return. Congress and the judiciary penetrated the internal mechanism of executive power. In any other democratic polity, it is inconceivable that the chief of the political executive could be compelled to yield tapes of private conversations either to a legislative or a judicial agency. No executive anywhere can function effectively under those circumstances; no decision-making institution can withstand that kind of microscopic scrutiny. As a consequence of legislative and judicial intrusion into the confidential and previously sheltered area of executive deliberation, the institution of the presidency has been impaired.

Following precedents established and changes made in the 1970s, no president can do now what Franklin Roosevelt was able to do before World War II, to say nothing of Abraham Lincoln in 1861. The vital intelligence agency cannot protect its agents, keep its sources confidential, or engage in the unfortunately necessary covert operations that fall to the lot of such organizations in all nations. Through the Freedom of Information Act and the relentless probing of congressional committees and their staffs, the operations of the entire government are exposed to public gaze. Friendly foreign governments naturally refuse to share information with the Americans because it is impossible to keep such information and their sources confidential. One of the major objectives of the Soviet military, "destabilization" of the American intelligence arm, has been achieved for them by the Americans themselves.

27

'Well, it's the same foreign policy I had when I was governor of California'

The United States government is now in the position of formulating and implementing foreign policy only in the full glare of publicity, while its opponents are free to promote their interests both in public forums and by stealth. When secrets are impossible to keep and open intervention equally impossible to mount, the result is a power vacuum. The balance of power is bound to tilt in favor of the side that can use military force with impunity.

The American political system functions poorly when the executive is weak. The logic of the system requires the president to act, subject to evaluation and criticism by an independent Congress. The legislative branch is not organized for the purpose of taking initiatives. Insertion of congressional power into the process of executive deliberation and decision making is like so many rods poking into the cogs of a mechanism. If the president is rendered incapable of providing a firm lead, there will be no firm lead at all. The complex system will spin its wheels in the air, which is precisely what has been happening since 1972...

Reducing the power of Congress, or rather restoring Congress to its legislative role, will be immensely difficult. Public opinion will have to be prepared for a change by events of the magnitude of the Vietnam War — or perhaps the German conquest of Western Europe in 1940; that is, only a catastrophe perceived as such by the American people will induce Congress to give up the power it assumed after Watergate — power institutionalized through the great expansion of its own bureaucracy.

PLAYING WITH LOADED DICE

The Vietnam and Watergate syndromes have loaded the dice in favor of defeat; the losing number is now bound to come up most of the time. It turned out that the American government was preparing — for six long and agonizing months — a military solution to the Iranian crisis. But the gods of war do not smile on the weak and the hesitant. The American government had to plan and undertake a commando operation with an intelligence agency and armed forces thoroughly demoralized by recruitment problems, shortages of trained personnel, and serious deficiencies in the maintenance of sophisticated equipment. Let us not be too critical of President Carter. Defeat is sometimes the bitter lot of democracies, as in the dark days of 1941 and 1942. But why was it necessary for the American president to announce the failure of the commando operation while the burned out helicopters were still smoldering and while American agents were still on Iranian soil? No other democracy in the world would have felt compelled to reveal those details so soon and so fully because no other democracy carries the burden of the Watergate syndrome. Only in the United States is it assumed that state secrets (America's, not others') are evil, that the press must know all and reveal all, that confidential conversations within the executive branch must be made public...

For the past decade the American people have had neither collective discipline nor a sense of national honor; and they have deprived themselves of the instruments of effective governance. As long as that situation endures, they will have no peace.

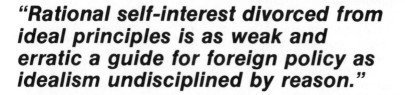

"Rational self-interest divorced from ideal principles is as weak and erratic a guide for foreign policy as idealism undisciplined by reason."

Idealism Should Guide Our Policy

Robert Endicott Osgood

Robert Endicott Osgood is an educator who has been Dean of the Johns Hopkins School of Advanced International Studies since 1973. A Harvard University PhD, he has served as Director of the Washington Center for Foreign Policy Research. Dr. Osgood's publications include *Alliances and American Foreign Policy* (1968) and the critically acclaimed *Retreat From Empire* (1973). In the following viewpoint, he contends that moral ideals must provide the basis for American foreign policy if America is to win the trust and admiration of the world which leadership requires.

Consider the following questions while reading:
1. Why does the author feel that it would harm our country internally to ignore moral principles in making foreign policy decisions?
2. Dr. Osgood claims that Americans are unable to make foreign policy decisions solely on the basis of self interest. What is his reasoning?
3. Why does the author feel that idealism is as much an instrument of national power as weapons of war?

Robert Endicott Osgood, *Ideals and Self-Interest in America's Foreign Relations.* (University of Chicago Press, 1953). Copyright 1953 by the University of Chicago.

SELF-INTEREST WITHOUT IDEALS IS
SELF-DEFEATING

If one assumes the worth of the Christian–liberal–humani-tarian ideals, as this essay does, then it is relevant to understand that the calculation and pursuit of national self-interest without regard for universal ideals is not only immoral but self–defeating...

If American power becomes an end in itself, American society, no less than international society, will suffer; for unless American security is measured by ideal standards transcending the national interest, it may take forms that undermine the moral basis of all social relations. If the Christian, humanitarian, and democratic values, which are the basis of America's social and political institutions, are valid at all, they are as valid outside American borders as within. Consequently, if they cease to compel respect in America's foreign relations, they will, ultimately, become ineffective in her domestic affairs. The resulting destruction of America's moral fiber through the loss of national integrity and the disintegration of ethical standards would be as great a blow to the nation as an armed attack upon her territory...

MORALITY MUST GUIDE US

"It is a very perilous thing to determine the foreign policy of a nation in the terms of material interest. It not only is unfair to those with whom you are dealing, but it is degrading as regards your own actions...

We dare not turn from the principle that morality and not expediency is the thing that must guide us and that we will never condone iniquity because it is most convenient to do so."

President Woodrow Wilson at Mobile, Alabama, October 27, 1913.

A view of international relations which imagines that nations can in the long run achieve a stable and effective foreign policy solely by a rational calculation of the demands of national self–interest is based upon an unrealistic conception of human nature, for it is certainly utopian to expect any great number of people to have the wit to perceive or the will to follow the dictates of enlightened self-interest on the basis of sheer reason alone. Rational self-interest divorced from ideal principles is as weak and erratic a guide for foreign policy as idealism undisciplined by reason. No great mass of people is Machiavellian, least of all the American people. Americans in particular have displayed a strong aversion to the pursuit of self-interest, unless self-interest has been leavened with moral sentiment.

A genuine realist should recognize that the transcendent ideals expressed in the traditional American mission, no less than America's fundamental strategic interest, are an indispensable source of stability in America's foreign relations...

THE EXPEDIENCY OF IDEALISM

A true realist must recognize that ideals and self-interest are so closely interdependent that, even on grounds of national expediency, there are cogent arguments for maintaining the vitality of American idealism.

Ideals are as much an instrument of national power as the weapons of war. All manifestations of national power, including the threat of coercion, operate by influencing the thoughts and actions of human beings, whether by frightening them or by converting them. Since men are motivated by faith and moral sentiment as well as by fear and the instinct of self-preservation, the strength of America's moral reputation and the persuasiveness of the American mission are as vital a factor in the power equation as planes, ships, and tanks. One has only to recall the consequences of the rise and fall of America's moral reputation during and after World War I to understand the force of American idealism among foreign peoples.

The persuasiveness of the American mission is especially significant under the present circumstances, when the competition of ideologies is such a conspicuous feature of the power struggle between the Russian and the American orbits and when the effectiveness of American policy depends so heavily upon winning the moral and intellectual allegiance of vast numbers of people in the throes of social and nationalistic revolution. If in the eyes of millions of people living in underdeveloped areas of the world the United States ceases to stand for a positive and constructive program of social and material progress, if American ideals no longer mean anything beyond smug generalities and hypocritical rationalizations of selfish national advantage, then all the wealth and military power the United States can muster will not render these people an asset to the free world. If the nations within the Western Coalition conclude that America has lost all passion for improving the lot of common people for the sake of the people themselves, if they believe that Americans have lost interest in the vision of world peace in their over-riding

"Oh wad some power the giftie gie us to see oursels as others see us"
—Robert Burns

Burck in the *Chicago Sun - Times*. Reprinted with permission from the *Chicago Sun-Times*.

concern for their national self-interest, then no display of shrewd power politics will win for the United States the popular trust and admiration which American leadership requires.

Moreover, no coalition can survive through a common fear of tyranny without a common faith in liberty. If the leader of the Western Coalition ceases to sustain that faith, then who will sustain it? Because the United States is unavoidably thrust into a position of global leadership, her standards of conduct must, inevitably, have a great influence in setting the moral tone of international relations in general. Consequently, it behooves America to conduct its foreign relations in a way that will encourage the kind of international environment compatible with its ideals and interests.

VIEWPOINT 4

"The safest basis for foreign policy lies not in attempts to determine what is right or wrong but in attempts to determine the national interest."

National Interests Should Guide Our Policy

Arthur Schlesinger, Jr.

A Special Assistant to the President of the United States from 1961 to 1964, Arthur Schlesinger, Jr. is currently Schweitzer Professor of Humanities at City University of New York. His books include *Robert Kennedy and His Times* (1978). In the following viewpoint, Mr. Schlesinger argues that to incorporate morality into a nation's foreign policy can eventually lead to fanaticism.

Consider the following questions while reading:
1. **Does Mr. Schlesinger feel that moral principles should have been involved in our decision to fight in Vietnam?**
2. **Why does the author believe that nations are not bound by the same moral principles that bind individuals? Do you agree?**
3. **What danger of fanaticism does Mr. Schlesinger see in nations whose foreign policy decisions are made on a moral basis?**

Arthur Schlesinger, Jr., "The Necessary Amorality of Foreign Affairs," *Harpers*, August, 1971. Copyright ©1971 by Minneapolis Star and Tribune Company, Inc. Reprinted by permission of the author.

For centuries, theologians have distinguished between just and unjust wars, jurists have propounded rules for international conduct, and moralists have worried whether their own nation's course in foreign affairs was right or wrong. Yet the problem of the relationship between morality and international politics remains perennially unsettled. It is particularly difficult and disturbing for Americans today. The Indochina war was first widely justified on moral grounds and then widely condemned on moral grounds. Both judgments cannot be right. This contradiction and, even more, of course, the shame and horror of the war must surely compel us to look again at the moral question in its relation to foreign policy...

Should — as both supporters and critics of the Indochina war asserted — overt moral principles decide issues of foreign policy? Required to give a succinct answer, I am obliged to say: as little as possible. If, in the management of foreign affairs, decisions can be made and questions disposed of on other grounds, so much the better. Moral values in international politics — or so, at least, my temperament enjoins me to believe — should be decisive only in questions of last resort. One must add that questions of last resort do exist...

THE MORALITY OF INDIVIDUALS AND OF STATES

The argument for the application of moral principles to questions of foreign policy is thus that there is, or should be, an identity between the morality of individuals and the morality of states. The issues involved here are not easy. Clearly, there are cases in foreign affairs where moral judgment is possible and necessary. But I suggest that these are extreme cases and do not warrant the routine use of moral criteria in making foreign-policy decisions. It was to expose such indiscriminate moralism that Reinhold Niebuhr wrote *Moral Man and Immoral Society* over forty years ago. The passage of time has not weakened the force of his analysis.

Niebuhr insisted on the distinction between the moral behavior of individuals and of social groups. The obligation of the individual was to obey the law of love and sacrifice; "from the viewpoint of the author of an action, unselfishness must remain the criterion of the highest morality." But nations cannot be sacrificial. Governments are not individuals. They are trustees for individuals. Niebuhr quotes Hugh Cecil's argument that unselfishness "is inappropriate to the action of a state. No one has a right to be unselfish with other people's interests." Alexander Hamilton made the same point in the early years of the American republic: "The rule of morality ... is

Is this the real Uncle Sam?

Justus in the *Minneapolis Star*. Reprinted with permission from the *Minneapolis Star*.

not precisely the same between nations as between individuals. The duty of making its own welfare the guide of its actions is much stronger upon the former than upon the latter. Existing millions, and for the most part future generations, are concerned in the present measures of a government; while the consequences of the private action of an individual ordinarily terminate with himself, or are circumscribed with a narrow compass."

NATION'S DUTY OF SELF-PRESERVATION

In short, the individual's duty of self-sacrifice and the

nation's duty of self-preservation are in conflict; and this makes it impossible to measure the action of nations by a purely individualistic morality. "The Sermon on the Mount," said Churchill, "is the last word in Christian ethics... Still, it is not on those terms that Ministers assume their responsibilities of guiding states." Saints can be pure, but statesmen must be responsible. As trustees for others, they must defend interests and compromise principles. In politics, practical and prudential judgment must have priority over moral verdicts...

A nation's law can set down relatively clear standards of right and wrong in individual behavior because it is the product of an imperfect but nonetheless authentic internal moral consensus. International life has no such broad or deep moral consensus. It was once hoped that modern technology would create a common fund of moral ideas transcending the interests of particular nations—common concepts of interest, justice, and comity—either because the revolution in communications would bring people together through hope of mutual understanding or because the revolution in weapons would bring them together through fear of mutual destruction. Such expectations have been disappointed. Until nations come to adopt the same international morality, there can be no world law to regulate the behavior of states. Nor can international institutions—the League of Nations or the United Nations—produce by sleight of hand a moral consensus where none exists. World law must express world community; it cannot create it...

It is not only that moral principles are of limited use in the conduct of foreign affairs. It is also that the compulsion to see foreign policy in moral terms may have, with the noblest of intentions, the most ghastly of consequences. The moralization of foreign affairs encourages, for example, a misunderstanding of the nature of foreign policy. Moralists tend to prefer symbolic to substantive politics.

They tend to see foreign policy as a means not of influencing events but of registering virtuous attitudes. One has only to recall the attempt, made variously by Right and Left, to make recognition policy an instrument of ethical approval or disapproval.

A QUESTION OF MORAL SUPERIORITY

A deeper trouble is inherent in the very process of pronouncing moral judgment of foreign policy. For the man who converts conflicts of interest and circumstance into conflicts of good and evil necessarily invests himself with moral superiority. Those who see foreign affairs as made up of questions of right and wrong begin by supposing they know better than other people what is right for them. The more passionately they believe they are right, the more likely they are to reject expediency and accommodation and seek the final victory of their principles. Little has been more pernicious in international politics than excessive righteousness...

Moralism in foreign policy ends up in fanaticism, and the fanatic, as Mr. Dooley puts it, "does what he thinks th' Lord wud do if He only knew th' facts in th' case." Abroad it leads to crusades and the extermination of the infidel; at home it perceives mistakes in political judgment as evidence of moral obliquity. The issue becomes not self-delusion or stupidity but criminality and treachery; ferreting out the reprobate as traitors or war criminals becomes the goal. Those who are convinced of their own superior righteousness should recall Chekhov's warning: "You will not become a saint through other people's sins."

WE MUST PROTECT OUR NATIONAL INTERESTS

There is, first of all, only one rational basis on which to base a foreign policy and that is the national interest of the United States. That seems obvious, but American decision-makers seem to think it is a cardinal sin to even consider our interests...

It is in our national interest that certain nations, because of their strategic location or because of their resources, not align themselves with the Soviet Union. Therefore it is in our national interest to support anti-communist governments and to oppose attempts to overthrow them by forces which are aligned with communism.

Charley Reese, *Manchester Union Leader*, February 6, 1981.

If moral principles have only limited application to foreign policy, then we are forced to the conclusion that decisions in foreign affairs must generally be taken on other than moral-

40

istic grounds. What are these other grounds?...

The safest basis for foreign policy lies not in attempts to determine what is right or wrong but in attempts to determine the national interest...

NATIONAL INTEREST AS MAINSPRING OF POLICY

A moment's thought will show that every nation *must* respond to some sense of its national interest, for a nation that rejects national interest as the mainspring of its policy cannot survive. Without the magnetic compass of national interest, there would be no regularity and predictability in national affairs. George Washington called it "a maxim founded on the universal experience of mankind that no nation is to be trusted farther than it is bound by its interest."...

National interest has a self–limiting factor. It cannot, unless transformed by an injection of moral righteousness, produce ideological crusades for unlimited objectives. Any consistent defender of the idea of national interest must concede that other nations have legitimate interests too, and this sets bounds on international conflict. "You can compromise interests," Hans Morgenthau has reminded us, "but you cannot compromise principles."...

Uncontrolled national egoism generally turns out to be contrary to long–term national interest. Can it be persuasively held, for example, that Hitler's foreign policy was in the national interest of Germany? The imperialist states of nineteenth–century Europe have generally been forced to revise their notions as to where national interest truly lies. In time this may even happen to the Soviet Union and the United States.

National interest, realistically construed, will promote enlightened rather than greedy policy. So a realist like Hamilton said (my emphasis) that his aim was not "to recommend a policy absolutely selfish or interested in nations; but to show, that a policy regulated by their own interest, *as far as justice and good faith permit,* is, and ought to be, their prevailing one." And a realist like Theodore Roosevelt could say: "It is neither wise nor right for a nation to disregard its own needs, and it is foolish—and maybe wicked—to think that other nations will disregard theirs. But it is wicked for a nation only to regard its own interest, and foolish to believe that such is the sole motive that actuates any other nation. It should be our steady aim to raise the ethical standard of national action just as we strive to raise the ethical standard of individual action."

"The profession of arms is the foundation on which this nation and every other great nation rests."

The Military Is Our Nation's Backbone

Charley Reese

Charley Reese is a syndicated columnist who learned his craft by working for several newspapers and by writing on subjects from sports to national politics. He is a member of the editorial board and a columnist for the *Sentinel Star,* Orlando, Florida, where he has worked since 1971. Mr. Reese has received several Associated Press honors and has been nominated for the Pulitzer Prize. In the following viewpoint, he claims that the rise and fall of nations is directly related to the rise and fall of their military strength.

Consider the following questions while reading:
1. **How does the author respond to the concept that ideas and words are more powerful than guns?**
2. **What "great evil" does the author think emerged from the Vietnam war? Do you agree?**

Charley Reese, "Foundation of Our Country," *Manchester Union Leader,* June 27, 1980. Reprinted by permission of the author.

One of the aspects of our society which drives me batty is that we seem so often to be totally disconnected to the realities of the world. There is no better illustration of this than the attitude many Americans display toward the military.

You see people who obviously view the military as a nuisance or a necessary evil at best. Others display open hostility. The movies and television and even journalists often portray the military as an institution of buffoons and maniacs.

This is not only plain wrong, but stupid.

THE FOUNDATION OF OUR COUNTRY

The profession of arms is the foundation on which this nation and every other great nation rests. You can analyze the causes of the rise and fall of nations but always and in every instance the immediate cause of both the rise and fall is the military strength or lack of military strength.

Intellectuals are fond of saying that ideas or words are more powerful than guns and bayonets. That is false. The only power ideas and words have is the power to motivate men to take up arms. Whatever is accomplished, however, is accomplished by the military.

The Declaration of Independence was signed in 1776. The real independence of the nation was established by the army and the navy. The independence of this nation has been maintained ever since by the military.

The free press, the arts, education, industry—everything we value in a society is dependent upon its survival on the military. We live blissfully inside a ring of iron. It has always been so and it will always be so. The destiny of the United States will not be determined by politicians or writers or educators but by the men and women in the Army, Navy, Marines, Air Force and Coast Guard.

Switzerland's famous neutrality is maintained by one of the most highly-trained, well-equipped armies in Europe. Neutral Switzerland has a draft and an extensive reserve system. Swiss reservists keep their weapons and ammunition in their homes so they will be ready for swift mobilization. The Swiss are neither stupid nor unrealistic.

A rational citizen who understands how dependent he is on the military appreciates the profession. He will not turn his back on them. He will not let the military be abused or insulted without defending them. He will pressure the politicians to provide the military with the manpower and equipment it needs. He will teach his children that it is an honor and a duty to serve in the armed forces. He will insist that the public school system do its part to teach children the value of the military by making them aware of its accomplishments and its heroes.

©1980, *St. Louis Globe - Democrat*. Reprinted with permission Los Angeles Times Syndicate.

VIETNAM PROPAGANDA

The great evil which emerged from the Vietnam War was allowing our enemies to wage a propaganda campaign inside our own country while our military forces were engaged in combat.

People who do not understand what Jane Fonda was about and is still about are so dumb they deserve the fate she has in mind for them. The woman should be in prison. I wouldn't throw a bucket of slop on her if she were on fire much less allow her image on my television screen or pay to see one of her propaganda films.

When Jane's friends took Da Nang, they lined up over 300 children ten and under who were in an orphanage run by our Marines. They set up machine guns and they killed them.

I suggest that you look at your own children or grandchildren and understand that the only thing that can keep them from a similar fate is the Armed Forces of the United States. Appreciate the American military? We'd better love it as we love our own lives.

"Power exposes us to the same temptation to ruthlessness, lawlessness, hypocrisy, and vanity to which all great powers were exposed in the past."

The Hypocrisy Of American Foreign Policy

Henry Steele Commager

Henry Steele Commager has been Simpson Lecturer at Amherst College since 1972. A historian and educator, he earned his MA and PhD degrees from the University of Chicago and holds many honorary degrees. Dr. Commager is the author of numerous books including *The Discipline of History* (1972) and is currently editing a fifty volume work entitled *The Rise of the American Nation*. In the following viewpoint, he warns that those who support the use of a double standard in American foreign policy are contributing to the weakening of democracy and liberty.

Consider the following questions while reading:
1. **What criticism does Dr. Commager have of America's westward expansion during our early history?**
2. **The author suggests that communism has corrupted American society. What is his point?**

Henry Steele Commager, "A Historian Looks at Our Political Morality," *Saturday Review,* July 10, 1965. Copyright 1965 Saturday Review, Inc. Reprinted with the permission of Saturday Review, Inc. and the author.

"Every philosophy," wrote Alfred North Whitehead, "is tinged with the coloring of some secret, imaginative background, which never emerges explicitly in its train of reasoning." True enough—though never is a pretty strong word here. What is the secret, or perhaps the inarticulate imaginative background, that colors American thinking about relations with other peoples and nations in the past and today? Is it not the once explicit and openly avowed, but now implicit assumption of American superiority, both material and moral, especially to lesser breeds without our law? Is it not the assumption that America is somehow outside the workings of history, exempt from such laws as may govern history?

ORIGIN OF ATTITUDE OF SUPERIORITY

The origin of this attitude traces back to the generation that created the new nation and came to think of that nation as a people apart. It is rooted in the long-popular notion of New World innocence and Old World corruption, New World virtue and Old World vice, a notion that runs like a red thread through the whole of our literature from Benjamin Franklin to Henry James, and through our politics and diplomacy as well. It is connected with the convulsive fact of physical removal— the uprooting and transplanting to new and more fertile soil, with the phenomenon of a continuous westward emigration from the Old World, while so few went eastward across the ocean. It is related to the American priority in independence and in nation-making, with the glowing achievements of the new nation—religious freedom, for example, the end to colonialism, the classless society—and over the years it was strengthened by the argument of special destiny, and by the experience of abundance and freedom from Old World wars, and of growth even beyond the dreams of the Founding Fathers. No wonder the notion of a special providence and a special destiny caught the American imagination.

Something was to be said for all this in the early years of the Republic, when the American world was not only new but brave. Rather less was to be said for it as the nineteenth century wore on—the century that saw the new nation indulge in so many of the follies of the older nations: slavery, racial and religious intolerance, the disparity between rich and poor, civil war, imperialism, and foreign wars.

But in the nineteenth century, perhaps especially in the nineteenth century, Americans developed the habit of brushing aside whatever was embarrassing that still characterizes them, the habit of taking for granted a double standard of history and morality. There were, to be sure, awkward things in our history, but somehow they were not to be held against us. Somehow they didn't count. The conquest and decimation of the Indian didn't count—after all, the Indians were heathens—and when that argument lost its force, there was the undeniable charge that they got in the way of progress. The students of my own college celebrate Lord Jeffrey Amherst on all ceremonial occasions, but few of them remember that Lord Amherst's solution to the Indian problem

Henry Steele Commager

was to send the Indians blankets infected with smallpox! How many of us, after all, remember what Helen Hunt Jackson called a "Century of Dishonor"? Or there was slavery; it was pervasive and flourishing, and slaveholders defended it as a moral good. Somehow slavery didn't count, either, because it was nature's way of bringing the African to Western civilization, or because it was all so romantic (only recently have we developed a sense of guilt here).

AMERICAN MANIFEST DESTINY

The Industrial Revolution, too, brought in its train most of the evils that afflicted Europe in these same stormy years, but that could all be put down as the price of progress, which is just what Herbert Spencer and his infatuated American followers did. And surely no one could assert that the price was too high. So, too, with what, in other nations, would be called imperialism, but with us was called "westward expansion" — manifest destiny working itself out in some foreordained fashion. The Mexicans do not take quite this view of the matter, but that has not troubled us. Even now we do not inquire quite as closely into the war–guilt question for the Mexican War, or the war with Spain, or the Filipino war, as we do for the Franco–Prussian War or World War I...

We are no longer quite so sure of the New World innocence and Old World corruption as in the past — sometimes we suspect it may be the other way around — but the older notions of American superiority, and of the exemption of America from the familiar processes of history persist. They were very much in the mind of Woodrow Wilson when he prepared to make the world safe for democracy. But then the world we made did not suit us at all; clearly we had been betrayed by the wicked diplomats of the Old World. We cut our losses and withdrew into isolation and watched the Old World destroy itself with a kind of malign satisfaction, meanwhile congratulating ourselves that we were not involved and that our irresponsibility was really a form of moral superiority.

A BIASED LOOK AT HISTORY

For we were very sure of our own virtue, and we read history to discover that we were a peculiar people. Our history books exalted everything American. They contrasted our Indian policy with the wicked policy of the Spaniards — that was part of the black legend — conveniently overlooking the elementary fact that the Indian survived in Mexico and South America but not in the United States. They painted slavery as a romantic institution, or perhaps as a kind of fortunate acci-

Hmm, 60,000 political prisoners – you qualify for U.S. aid

dent for the Africans. They even ascribed the exceeding bounty of nature not to providence or to luck but to our own virtue. In recent years, many of our spokesmen commit the vulgar error of identifying an economy based on unrestricted exploitation of natural abundance as "the American way of life," and of scorning less fortunate people for having fewer resources and a different, and obviously inferior, way of life. We forget Reinhold Niebuhr's admonishment that "The more

51

we indulge in uncritical reverence for the supposed wisdom of the American way of life, the more odious we make it in the eyes of the world, and the more we destroy our moral authority..."

During the great war we responded, generously and unselfishly, to the challenge that confronted us; this was, in a sense, our finest hour, too: Lend-Lease, the alliance with Britain, the acceptance of the Soviet as an ally in the struggle against tyranny, the Atlantic Charter and the United Nations and the far-sighted Marshall Plan, the response to the challenge of aggression in Korea. But the rising threat of Communism did what the actual attack by Nazi and Fascist powers had been unable to do. The prolonged struggle with Communism, which we sometimes call the Cold War, accentuated our innate sense of superiority. To vast numbers of Americans it justified—and apparently still does justify—resort to almost any weapons or conduct. For years now we have heard, and not from extremists alone, that the struggle between democracy and Communism is the struggle between Light and Darkness, Good and Evil, and that the moral distinction is an absolute one.

The arguments that were invoked to justify religious wars and religious persecution in past centuries are invoked now to justify sleepless hostility to Communism—even preventive war. Happily, the extremists have not had their way in the conduct of foreign policy, but we know how effective they have been on the domestic scene, how they have denounced as traitors those who do not agree with them and persecuted them with relentless venom, how they have poisoned public life, and private, too, preaching hatred of Russia, hatred of Cuba, hatred of China—hatred directed toward all those who do not agree with them and with their easy remedies. Those hate-mongers, sure of themselves and of their moral superiority, have not hesitated to ignore law and the Constitution when it suited their book or to lie and cheat and betray in what they complacently assumed was a good cause because they espoused it.

SPREADING THE GOSPEL OF HATRED

Those who cultivate and spread the gospel of hatred throughout our society bear a heavy responsibility. They do not really weaken Communism; they weaken democracy and liberty. By their conduct and their philosophy they lower the moral standards of the society they pretend to defend. Eager to put down imagined subversion, they are themselves the most subversive of all the elements in our society, for they subvert "that harmony and affection" without which a society cannot be a commonwealth.

Much of our current foreign policy takes once again the form of indulgence in a double standard of morality. Thus it is contrary to international law to make reconnaissance flights over the territory of another nation—the Soviet reminded us of that a few years back—but we make such flights over Cuba and China: if Cuban planes flew over Florida or Chinese over Hawaii we might take a less easygoing view of the matter. We justly condemn Nazi destruction of Rotterdam and Warsaw, cities that were not military objectives, but we conveniently forget that we were chiefly responsible for the senseless destruction of Dresden—not a military object—within a few weeks of the end of the war, with a loss of 135,000 lives. It is a matter for rejoicing that we have the nuclear bomb, but when China detonated her first bomb our President told us that "this is a dark day in history." Perhaps so, though so far we are the only nation that has ever used the bomb—a fact which the Asians remember a bit better than we do...

THE AMERICAN INCONSISTENCY

Isn't there a certain amount of hypocrisy in proclaiming democracy and equal rights and opportunities for all at home, on the one hand, and assuming that other countries will do our bidding in the international system, on the other?

There is at least an inconsistency between the principles of the American system and the way we behave in international relations. Whether it gnaws at us internally or not, the inconsistency is certainly seen by others outside the U.S. and generates suspicion, distrust, and sometimes hatred, which we then, of course, can not understand.

Llewellyn D. Howell, *USA Today,* January, 1981.

A FURTHER LOOK AT THE DOUBLE STANDARD

When the Russians announced that they would not tolerate an unfriendly government in Hungary, and sent their troops and tanks crashing into that country in 1956, we were rightly enraged, but we think it quite right for us to announce that we will not tolerate an unfriendly regime in Santo Domingo and to send 20,000 Marines to "restore order" in that island. We complain, and rightly, that other countries do not abide by their international agreements, but we are ready to forgive ourselves for brushing aside international agreements when we face something we regard as an "emergency."

We have always criticized secret diplomacy—remember President Wilson's crusade—but when the CIA operates with such secrecy that even our own government is apparently taken by surprise, that just shows how clever we are. For the Russians or the Chinese to stir up revolution in other lands is subversive of international order, but when we encourage a coup d'etat or a revolution—from Iran to Brazil to Vietnam—it is all in a good cause.

We have not of late heard quite so much as some months back of what must surely be counted the ultimate arrogance —the cry of the "better dead than Red" crusaders. Those highly vocal martyrs are so sure that they are quite ready to condemn to extinction not only themselves and their fellow citizens, but the rest of the world and all potential posterity.

It is three-quarters of a century now since Lord Acton made the famous pronouncement that all power tends to corrupt and that absolute power corrupts absolutely. We had thought, and hoped, that we were exempt from this rule, but it is clear that we are not. Power exposes us to the same temptation to ruthlessness, lawlessness, hypocrisy, and vanity to which all great powers were exposed in the past.

In a simpler day we could survive this threat of corruption without serious damage. We could count on wearing out the brief spell of violence and corruption, or on circumscribing its effects. But now that we are a world power and our conduct affects the fate of every nation on the globe, we can no longer afford this piece of self-indulgence. Now we must square our conduct with principles of law and of morality that will withstand the scrutiny of public opinion everywhere and the tests of history as well.

RECOGNIZING ETHNOCENTRIC STATEMENTS

Ethnocentrism is the attitude or tendency of people to view their race, religion, culture, group, or nation as superior to others, and to judge others on that basis. An American, whose custom is to eat with a fork or spoon, would be making an ethnocentric statement when saying, "The Chinese custom of eating with chopsticks is stupid."

Ethnocentrism has promoted much misunderstanding and conflict. It emphasizes cultural and religious differences and the notion that one's national institution's or group's customs are superior.

Ethnocentrism limits people's ability to be objective and to learn from others. Education in the truest sense stresses the similarities of the human condition throughout the world and the basic equality and dignity of all people.

Consider each of the following statements carefully. Mark E for any statement you think is ethnocentric. Mark N for any statement you think is not ethnocentric. Mark U if you are undecided about any statement.

E = Ethnocentric
N = Not Ethnocentric
U = Undecided

_____ 1. The people of Iran are not fully capable of governing themselves without some assistance from Western countries.

_____ 2. We are a proud nation, with much in our history of which to be rightly proud.

_____ 3. Many societies are not ready for civil liberties and parliamentary democracy because the necessary social and economic conditions are lacking.

_____ 4. The U.S. leads the world in doing the impossible. History reflects no other national progress of such dimension. America must preserve a heritage that proved the soundness of Western culture.

_____ 5. Since Fidel Castro established communism in Cuba, he has spared no effort to expand communism to the rest of Latin America.

_____ 6. Every time the communists conquer a country anywhere in the world, the danger of war is created.

_____ 7. As an economic system capitalism is far superior to communism.

_____ 8. In some cases, communism may be considered a fairer economic alternative to capitalism.

_____ 9. You can't trust the Russians.

_____ 10. God has been preparing the Christian world for two thousand years to bring spiritual and social justice to all the world.

_____ 11. America is God's chosen country.

_____ 12. The United States is the world's largest food producing country.

_____ 13. The external force eroding democracy in Latin America is the United States.

BIBLIOGRAPHY

The following list of periodical articles deals with the subject matter of this chapter.

Arnaud de Borchgrave — *A Strong America: Key to World Peace,* **New Guard,** Winter, 1980-81, p. 30.

Thomas Buergenthal — *Human Rights and the U.S. National Interests: We Must Be Ideologically Neutral,* **Vital Speeches of the Day,** April 15, 1981, p. 414.

Stephen Cohen — *Wrong on Human Rights,* **The New Republic,** March 28, 1981, p. 13.

Norman Cousins — *History Lesson,* **Saturday Review,** May 12, 1979, p. 12.

William R. Hawkins — *Armed Intervention and Foreign Policy,* **New Guard,** Winter, 1979-80, p. 36.

William P. Hoar — *It's Time for a Tough American Policy,* **American Opinion,** April, 1981, p. 25.

Leon Howell — *Human Rights Emphasis Essential to U.S. Role in Global Events,* **engage/social action,** July/August, 1981, p. 29.

Llewellyn D. Howell — *America's Role in the International Arena: Why Not Number Two?,* **USA Today,** January, 1981, p. 15.

Ramon H. Myers — *Options for American Foreign Policy in the 1980's,* **Vital Speeches of the Day,** February 1, 1981, p. 231.

Ronald Steel — *After the Binge,* **The New Republic,** February 14, 1981, p. 17.

Ronald Steel — *Foreign Policy Agenda,* **The New Republic,** January 24, 1981, p. 15.

The New Republic — *The Policy is Guns,* June 27, 1981, p. 5.

USA Today — *Pro and Con: Overhaul U.S. Policy on Human Rights,* March 2, 1981, p. 49.

Cyrus R. Vance — *U.S. Foreign Policy: Constructive Change,* **Vital Speeches of the Day,** July 1, 1980, p. 568.

Chapter

Is Communism a Threat?

"Thermonuclear war and surrender to communism are high on the list of the greatest tragedies that could befall this nation... These dangers are caused largely by the communist determination to impose communist power on the entire world."

The Communist Plan For Worldwide Domination

Fred Schwarz

Fred Schwarz participated in the formation of the Christian Anti-Communism Crusade in 1953 while attending the University of Queensland Medical School in Australia. In 1955, he closed his medical practice in Sydney so that he could devote full time to the Crusade as its president. Dr. Schwarz's books include *You Can Trust the Communists (To Be Communists)* and *The Three Faces of Revolution*.

Consider the following questions while reading:

1. **What formula does the author claim the communists are following to conquer the United States?**
2. **What is the Brezhnev Doctrine and how does it endanger the U.S.?**
3. **According to the author, what seven step plan do the communists use to enslave countries?**

The viewpoint above is excerpted from the November 15, 1980 issue of Christian Anti-Communist Crusade, edited by Fred Schwarz.

Thermonuclear war and surrender to communism are high on the list of the greatest tragedies that could befall this nation. Unfortunately, the possibility that one or the other may take place is very real.

If you wish to avert these tragedies, please read this letter carefully. It will describe both the rationale and the course of a program of effective action to prevent them...

These dangers are caused largely by the communist determination to impose communist power on the entire world. The communists believe, with great sincerity, that they have an inescapable historic mandate to do this. Their preferred method of achieving it is by surrender, but the possibility of thermonuclear war also exists.

The formula they are following to achieve the conquest of the United States is: *"External encirclement, plus internal demoralization, plus thermonuclear blackmail, lead to progressive surrender."* The communists hope and believe that actual thermonuclear war will probably prove unnecessary as the United States can be reduced to relative impotence by the continuing conquest of more and more countries throughout the world which will result in this country being deprived of material resources such as oil and strategic minerals which are essential for defense. However, if war eventuates, the Soviet Union is designing its weapons and strategies so that the war can be won.

THE MAIN WAR DANGER

Every time the communists conquer a country anywhere in the world, the danger of war is created. This is because of the Brezhnev Doctrine which is a practical application of the communist doctrine of Proletarian Internationalism, which teaches that a unity exists between the working men, or proletariat, of the entire world. The leaders of the Communist Party of the Soviet Union believe that they are the leaders of the world proletariat and that they have the responsibility of maintaining and extending the victories of the world proletariat. They believe that there is a law of history which is as definite as the law of gravity. One result of the law of gravity is that water runs downhill; and one result of the law of history is that every nation must move towards being ruled by communists. History must be obeyed, so the entire communist movement must assure that once communist power is established anywhere, it will be retained permanently. In obedience to this historic command, the Brezhnev Doctrine states that, if necessary, the military forces of international communism must be used to maintain communist power if the people of any country threaten to overthrow the communist rulers. The invading military forces of communism are always presented as giving fraternal assistance to the national communist leaders.

Thus, the conquest of any country anywhere by the communists creates the danger of Soviet military intervention

Fred Schwarz

and the possibility of a wider war. Soviet intervention in Afghanistan is the latest example of this.

It cannot be stressed too much that the danger of military conflict comes after the conquest of a country by the communists. With the exception of the countries of Eastern Europe at the end of the second world war, countries are not usually conquered for communism by external military power. They are conquered from within by national communist leaders. Here is the process by which this conquest takes place.

PATHWAY OF COMMUNIST CONQUEST

Countries have been conquered and are being conquered by the following steps:

1. The recruitment of individuals into the national communist party.

   Those who are recruited are usually idealistic students who see communism as a practical method to overcome the backwardness, poverty, injustice, and oppression that surrounds them. They see themselves as the creators and directors of a new tomorrow.

2. The training of these recruits so that they become obedient, disciplined, and efficient servants of the communist cause.

3. The equipment of these recruits with specially prepared literature which presents a glorious, but false, picture of life in communist–controlled countries. The communist recruits distribute this on a mass scale. This literature distribution is accompanied by broadcasts which glamorize communism and its international achievements and promise the people deliverance from the evils that beset them.

4. These communist recruits create a mass movement by exploiting the grievances of the people. They either create new organizations or infiltrate existing organizations in the political, educational, religious, and cultural realm.

5. The national communists are supported by international communists who provide direction, financial support, and essential equipment and who help through diplomatic maneuvers, skilled propaganda, misinformation, espionage, and blackmail.

THE LEFT HAND HAS NEVER BEEN RETRACTED

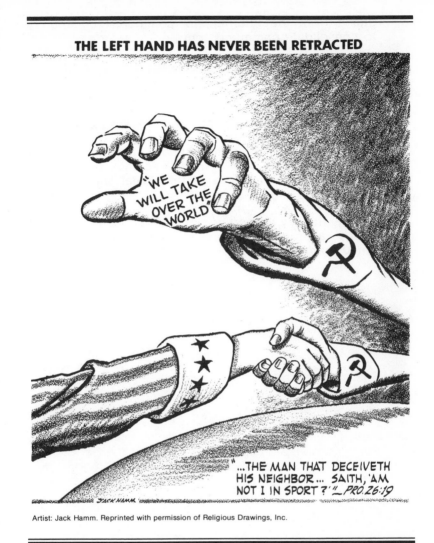

Artist: Jack Hamm. Reprinted with permission of Religious Drawings, Inc.

6. At the appropriate moment the attempt is made to seize political power. This may be done by seeking to win elections or, more commonly, by armed revolution.

7. Once installed in power, the communists monopolize all the mechanisms by which the people are controlled and establish their own dictatorship. If the people, who are disillusioned, appear to be making successful efforts to overthrow this dictatorship, military forces are intro-

duced from the international communist community to consolidate communist power.

Every time a country is conquered in this manner, it increases the encirclement of the United States and also increases the possibility of war.

If the communist conquest of the underdeveloped countries can be stopped, it stops the process of encirclement which is designed to lead to ultimate surrender. It also diminishes the danger of war which becomes a possibility every time the military forces of the Soviet Union invade another country.

Therefore, the key to averting both thermonuclear war and surrender is a program to prevent communist conquest of threatened countries.

"The sooner we focus on nations rather than ideologies, the sooner we can clarify precisely who and what is the real threat to the U.S."

World Communism Is Not a Threat

Vincent Davis

Vincent Davis is director of the Patterson School of Diplomacy and International Commerce at the University of Kentucky. In the following viewpoint, he contends that world communism is not the solid monolith many have pictured and that communism is subordinated to nationalism almost everywhere, including the USSR.

Consider the following questions while reading:
1. What example does Mr. Davis give to illustrate his contention that superpowers always regard one another as a threat?
2. According to the author, what is the most powerful "ism" in the world today?
3. What reasons does he give for the adversary relationship between the U.S. and the USSR?

Vincent Davis, "Communism Never Was the Enemy," *The Christian Science Monitor,* July 24, 1981. Reprinted by permission from *The Christian Science Monitor,* ©1981 The Christian Science Publishing Society. All rights reserved.

Hierarchies of status and authority have always existed in social systems. These pecking orders are inherent in all societies, and are established by pecking. In the international social system, nations peck on each other.

THE RIVALRY BETWEEN SUPERPOWERS

Superpowers have typically emerged after the pecking process has eliminated other possible contenders. World War I was one such process of elimination, with the United States and Britain remaining as the two logical superpower contenders. At least, President Wilson thought so soon after Armistice Day when he directed US military leaders to plan on Britain as America's most likely new enemy. Wilson had feared that the German fleet interned at Scapa Flow would be added to the Royal British Navy, although his anxieties were later eased when those formidable ships were scuttled.

The point is that, while the US and Britain probably were closer in terms of shared values and heritage than any other two nations on earth, this common ideological stance did not prevent the US from viewing Britain as the most likely new threat. Superpowers resemble rogue elephants in the forest — they regard each other warily simply because they are the only animals capable of doing great harm to one another, notwithstanding all other considerations.

In like manner, the US and the Soviet Union emerged from World War II as the two valid superpower contenders, and started pecking on each other. Ideological quarrels aggravated what was certain to be a major rivalry in any event, but those differences were not the main issue. Yet great confusion has existed among Americans for several decades as to whether their enemy was "communism" or the USSR.

THE CONFUSION OVER COMMUNISM

Navy Secretary Forrestal made an early contribution to this confusion during 1945–46 when he distributed within the Truman cabinet and elsewhere (including the Pope as one recipient) a paper prepared by a small "braintrust" on Forrestal's staff. Any presumptive superpower emerging victorious from a big war will characteristically look around and ask itself: are there any potential new enemies on the horizon? That's what Wilson did when he pinpointed Britain in late 1918. But, when Forrestal did it in 1945–46, he identified the USSR and then defined it in terms of communism.

This thing called communism was definitely America's big

scare in the 1950s. "Red" China had joined this threat complex, and it was assumed: (1) all communists are centrally directed; (2) all communists are the same; (3) once a communist, always a communist. We defined the "communist bloc" as a huge unbreakable chunk of granite about to start a

Justus in The Minneapolis Star

"There's the best vote-getter ever invented"

global avalanche which would destroy us—unless we could check it.

Secretary of State Dulles early in his tenure operated with the axiom: if you're not clearly with us, you're against us—and tantamount to being communist if not in fact so. Dulles at the end of his term had gained enough wisdom to reverse the formulation: if you're not clearly against us, maybe you could be with us. But the confusion remained.

Columbia University professor Zbigniew Brzezinski believed that the communist glue was strong enough to hold the pieces together regardless of other factors. Accordingly, he wrote in the April 1961 issue of Foreign Affairs that no such thing as a "Sino–Soviet split" could ever occur, while most knowledgeable specialists were agreeing that it had in fact occurred. Secretary of State Dean Rusk near the end of his term uttered the central truth: communism exists in as many different variations as there are countries in which it is found. Now we understand that there are important differences even within such countries.

THE MOST POWERFUL "ISM"

The most powerful "ism" in the world today and for at least 100 years has been nationalism. Communism almost everywhere—including the USSR—is subordinated to nationalism and national interests as nationally defined. Any definition of national interests, however, is always in flux, as national and international circumstances shift. Communism as such was never the enemy. We now have a combined intelligence operation with—think of it!—one of the two communist giants, China, to spy on the other one. Similarly, the USSR will do business with any country which can help it pursue its national interests, and it operates 84 capitalist profit-seeking companies worldwide.

America's dominant adversary is and has been the USSR, not because it is communist, but because it is the other superpower, armed to the teeth, willing to use aggression, operating a totalitarian system with traditional Russian values wholly contrary to the individualist values of the West. We can get along with a variety of leftist governments as long as they are independently and nonaggressively nationalistic—not just China, but Yugoslavia, Poland, Romania, and others. Yet a Reagan administration critic advises studying Marxism-Leninism before believing that the USSR is masterminding world terrorism, and the administration itself sees communism as the enemy south of the border.

THE UNRAVELING OF COMMUNISM

What emerges in the view of many Western analysts is a portrait of Communism in bankruptcy, a system ill-equipped to build or manage a modern economy. The Communist empire that emerged after World War II steadily unravels, with more nations emulating the independence of Yugoslavia...

Communism's ideological allure is waning, as well, falling victim to nationalism.

U.S. News & World Report, December 22, 1980.

The sooner we focus on nations rather than ideologies, the sooner we can clarify precisely who and what is the real threat to the US.

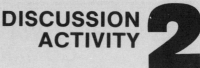

DISTINGUISHING BETWEEN FACT AND OPINION

This discussion activity is designed to help develop the *critical thinking skill of distinguishing between fact and opinion.* Consider the following quotation as an example. "Christianity is one of the major world religions and has had a profound influence upon the course of world history." The preceding statement is a fact which no historian or theologian, of any religious persuasion, would deny. But let us consider a statement which attempts to judge the influence of Christianity upon civilization. "The world would be a better place were it not for Christianity." Such a statement is clearly an expressed opinion. The good or bad effects Christianity has had, is having or will have upon humanity obviously depend upon one's point of view. An atheist will view Christianity from a far different perspective than will a devout Christian.

Instructions

Some of the following statements are taken from this book and some have other origins. Consider each statement carefully. Mark *O* for any statement you feel is an opinion or interpretation of facts. Mark *F* for any statement you believe is a fact. Then discuss and compare your judgments with those of other class members.

O = Opinion
F = Fact

_____ 1. The Third World has been looted by the West and especially by the United States.

_____ 2. The United States government is now in the position of formulating and implementing foreign policy only in the full glare of publicity, while its opponents are free to promote their interests both in public forums and by stealth.

_____ 3. The American political system functions poorly when the executive is weak.

_____ 4. The United States gives foreign aid to communist and non-communist countries.

_____ 5. The profession of arms is the foundation on which this nation and every other great nation rests.

_____ 6. The most powerful "ism" in the world today and for at least 100 years has been nationalism.

_____ 7. A foreign policy centered simply on anti-Sovietism makes no sense for the United States.

_____ 8. American foreign policy, like Russian foreign policy toward its satellite states, is rooted in arrogance.

_____ 9. Nations like Tanzania and Venezuela are not impoverished because of Northern Hemisphere affluence but because of their own internal inefficiencies and corruption.

_____ 10. The insurgency in El Salvador has been progressively transformed into another case of indirect armed aggression against a small Third World country by Communist powers acting through Cuba.

_____ 11. The U.S. should change its policy toward El Salvador to avert further disaster, both for Salvadoreans and for the United States.

_____ 12. Russia has the world's largest navy.

_____ 13. U.S. military spending has increased considerably in recent years.

"Communism is unregenerate; it will always present a mortal danger to mankind."

The Deadly Threat of Communism

Alexander Solzhenitsyn

Alexander Solzhenitsyn is probably the most famous and controversial Soviet exile in the world today. He spent over 10 years in Russian prisons for his criticism of the Soviet system. The winner of the Nobel Prize for Literature in 1970, Solzhenitsyn was finally exiled from the Soviet Union in 1974. His many books include *Detente: Prospects for Democracy and Dictatorship* (1976). In the following viewpoint, Solzhenitsyn claims that while the West denies the reality of communism's goal of world domination, communists envelop country after country.

Consider the following questions while reading:
1. **In the author's opinion, how does the West attempt to explain away the danger of communism?**
2. **How do the communists exploit "detente"?**
3. **What examples of communist exploitation does the author cite?**

Alexander Solzhenitsyn, "Solzhenitsyn on Communism," *Time*, February 18, 1980. Translated by Alexis Klimoff. ©1980 by Alexander Solzhenitsyn. Reprinted with permission.

The West began its perilous miscalculation of Communism in 1918: from the very beginning the Western powers failed to see the deadly threat that it represented...

Alexander Solzhenitsyn

The West often seeks an explanation for the phenomenon of 20th century Communism in some supposed defects of the Russian nation. This is ultimately a racist view. (How then can China be explained? Viet Nam? Cuba? Ethiopia? Or the likes of Georges Marchais?) Flaws are sought everywhere but in Communism itself. Its aggressiveness is explained by, for example, Averell Harriman, in terms of a national dread of foreign aggression; this is said to account for the building of a vast arsenal and the seizing of new countries.

Western diplomats depend on unsound hypotheses that involve supposed "left" and "right" factions of the Politburo, when, in reality, all of its members are united in seeking world conquest and are undiscriminating in the means they use. Insofar as struggles do occur within the Politburo, they are purely personal; they cannot be used for diplomatic leverage...

Try asking a malignant tumor what makes it grow. It simply cannot behave otherwise. The same is true of Communism; driven by a malevolent and irrational instinct for world domination, it cannot help seizing ever more lands. Communism is something new, unprecedented in world history; it is fruitless to seek analogies. All warnings to the West about the pitiless and insatiable nature of Communist regimes have proved to be in vain because the acceptance of such a view would be too terrifying...

For decades it has been standard practice to deny reality by citing "peaceful coexistence," "détente," "the Kremlin leadership's pursuit of peace." Meanwhile Communism envelops country after country and achieves new missile capabilities. Most amazing is that the Communists themselves have for decades loudly proclaimed their goal of destroying the bourgeois world (they have become more circumspect lately), while the West merely smiled at what seemed to be an extravagant joke. Yet destroying a class is a process that has already been demonstrated in the U.S.S.R. So has the method of exiling an entire people into the wilderness in the space of 24 hours.

Communism can implement its "ideals" only by destroying the core and foundation of the nation's life. He who understands this will not for a minute believe that Chinese Communism is more peace-loving than the Soviet variety (it is simply that its teeth have not yet grown), or that Marshal Tito's brand is kindly by nature. The latter was also leavened with blood, and it too consolidated its power by mass killings, but the weak-hearted West preferred not to take any notice in

74

COMMUNISM & DETENTE

Communism needs the whole charade of détente for only one purpose: to gain additional strength with the help of Western financing (those loans will not be repaid) and Western technology before it launches its next large-scale offensive. Communism is stronger and more durable than Nazism, it is far more sophisticated in its propaganda and excels at such charades.

Communism is unregenerate; it will always present a mortal danger to mankind. It is like an infection in the world's organism: it may lie dormant, but it will inevitably attack with a crippling disease. There is no help to be found in the illusion that certain countries possess an immunity to Communism: any country that is free today can be reduced to prostration and complete submission...

CUTTING OFF THE COMMUNISTS

American foreign policy should, at the very least, force the Reds to sink or swim on their own. It should then draw the line and cut off every Communist toe that intrudes upon it. The final step, and our long-term objective, must be to help the captive peoples to free themselves. And that includes the people of Russia as certainly as it does those of Cuba.

William P. Hoar, *American Opinion*, April, 1981.

Communism is inimical and destructive of *every* national entity. The American antiwar movement long nurtured the hope that in North Viet Nam nationalism and Communism were in harmony, that Communism seeks the national self-determination of its beloved people. But the grim flotilla of boats escaping from Viet Nam — even if we count only those that did not sink—may have explained to some less ardent members of the movement where the national consciousness resides and always did reside. The bitter torment of millions of dying Cambodians (to which the world is already growing accustomed) demonstrates this even more vividly. Take Poland: the nation prayed for just a few days with the Pope; only the blind could still fail to distinguish the people from Communism. Consider the Hungarian freedom fighters, the East Germans who keep on dying as they try to cross the Wall, and the Chinese who plunge into shark-infested waters in the hope of reaching Hong Kong. China conceals its secrets best of all; the West hastens to believe that this, at least, is "good, peace-loving" Communism. Yet the same unbridgeable abyss, the same hatred separate the Chinese regime and the Chinese people...

In expectation of World War III the West again seeks cover, and finds Communist China as an ally! This is another betrayal, not only of Taiwan, but of the entire oppressed Chinese people. Moreover, it is a mad, suicidal policy: having supplied billion-strong China with American arms, the West will defeat the U.S.S.R., but thereafter no force on earth will restrain Communist China from world conquest. We must make a stand.

THE LAST DOMINO!

Reprinted by permission from the Manchester Union Leader.

Communism stops only when it encounters a wall, even if it is only a wall of resolve. The West cannot now avoid erecting such a wall in what is already its hour of extremity. Meanwhile, however, 20 possible allies have fallen to Communism since World War II. Meanwhile, Western technology has helped develop the terrifying military power of the Communist world. The wall will have to be erected with what strength remains. The present generation of Westerners will have to make a stand on the road upon which its predecessors have so thoughtlessly retreated for 60 years.

"Communism as an ideology is dead or semi-dead. It isn't working. It has lost its attraction."

The Twilight of Communism

Roscoe Drummond

Roscoe Drummond is the Washington columnist for the Los Angeles Times Syndicate and *The Christian Science Monitor.* A noted lecturer, he earned his BSJ and LLD degrees from Syracuse University. In the following viewpoint, Mr. Drummond claims that a consensus exists among authorities on Soviet affairs that communism, as an ideology, is dead because it simply does not work.

Consider the following questions while reading:

1. Why does the author think that the influence of communism is declining? Do you agree?
2. Why does the author think that Russia will rely more on military force than it has in the past?

I have always tended to step back from writing too readily about what is now being discussed as the "twilight of communism" lest we falsely assume that our main anxiety is at the point of vanishing.

But enough has been happening in recent months to make it evident:

That international communism isn't what it used to be.

That the Soviet empire in Eastern Europe is in trouble.

That Marxist ideology is losing its attraction in much of the world.

That the survival of communist regimes, where they have been imposed by Moscow, are endangered by rising nationalism and frustration because Marxist economics are increasing poverty rather than decreasing it.

These are not merely random assessments. They constitute a considerable consensus among scholars who have devoted careers to studying Soviet affaris.

MARXISM DOES NOT WORK

Says Abraham Brumbert, former editor of Problems of Communism: "Whether or not the Poles succeed makes absolutely no difference. What is happening is perhaps the most serious turning point in Eastern Europe and perhaps in communism throughout the world. I think that Moscow will more and more become a symbol of just brute power, and it will cease to be the great ideology of the future."

Says Seweryn Bialer, author of numerous works on the Soviet Union: "Communism as an ideology is dead or semi-dead. It isn't working. It has lost its attraction."

Says Leslie Gelb, a former State Department specialist and now a research scholar with the Carnegie Endowment for International Peace: "When we look back at this year in history, it could turn out to be the beginning of a serious economic collapse of the Soviet bloc. Their system doesn't work."

The Economist of London goes so far as to say that Russia's economic problems "could be terminal."

Nearly all third-world countries, except those under Soviet domination, voted at the United Nations for a resolution calling on the Soviets to withdraw their forces from Afghanistan. Chairman Brezhnev couldn't sell the Afghan invasion even to Indira Gandhi.

The most important single event which gives shudders to the Soviet Union is that in Poland a unified working class has successfully challenged the Polish communist party's monopoly of political power. The working class is supposed to be the essential bastion of any communist government. Polish workers, now 10 million of them in independent unions, are setting out to shape the "dictatorship of the proletariat," not be dominated by it.

THE MYTH OF THE COMMUNIST MONOLITH

The master myth of the cold war is that the Communist bloc is a monolith composed of governments which are not really governments at all but organized conspiracies, divided among themselves perhaps in certain matters of tactics, but all equally resolute and implacable in their determination to destroy the free world...

The myth is that every Communist state is an unmitigated evil and a relentless enemy of the free world; the reality is that some Communist regimes pose a threat to the free world while others pose little or none, and that if we will recognize these distinctions, we ourselves will be able to influence events in the Communist bloc in a way favorable to the security of the free world.

J.W. Fulbright, former Senator, Arkansas.

The deteriorating Polish economic conditions and the inability of the Marxists to correct them, which touched off the latest revolt of the workers, prevail widely in other Soviet-ruled East European countries. This is a threat to the stability, perhaps to the very existence, of communist regimes wherever they have been imposed by outside force.

THE RELIANCE ON FORCE

The fact that Marxist ideology is waning in its appeal almost everywhere in the world, that China and Russia are at odds with each other, that the Soviet Union is immersed in multiple crises — these developments do not mean that the Kremlin is about to roll over and cry uncle or that the West may soon have little to worry about.

It means something quite different. It now must be clear to Moscow that with Marxism no longer an appealing commodity, it must rely almost totally on its military might to extend its presence and influence to other countries.

This is the primary reason the Soviet Union has been steadily expanding its military strength. This is a plausible reason why the Kremlin leaders refused to join President Carter in any effort to reduce radically their mutual stockpiles of strategic weapons.

If such a goal is ever achieved, we can relax — but not before.

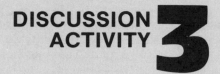
UNDERSTANDING STEREOTYPES

A stereotype is an oversimplified or exaggerated description of people or things. Stereotyping can be favorable. However, most stereotyping tends to be highly uncomplimentary and, at times, degrading.

Stereotyping grows out of our prejudices. When we stereotype someone, we are prejudging him or her. Consider the following example: Mr. X is convinced that all Mexicans are lazy, sloppy and careless people. The Diaz family, a family of Mexicans, happen to be his next-door neighbors. One evening, upon returning home from work, Mr. X notices that the garbage pails in the Diaz driveway are overturned and that the rubbish is scattered throughout the driveway. He immediately says to himself: "Isn't that just like those lazy, sloppy and careless Mexicans?" The possibility that a group of neighborhood vandals or a pack of stray dogs may be responsible for the mess never enters his mind. Why not? Simply because he has prejudged all Mexicans and will keep his stereotype consistent with his prejudice. The famous (or infamous) Archie Bunker of television fame is a classic example of our Mr. X.

Read through the following list carefully. Mark **S** for any statement that is an example of stereotyping. Mark **N** for any statement that is not an example of stereotyping. Mark **U** if you are undecided about any statement. Then discuss and compare your decisions with other class members.

S = **Stereotype**
N = **Not a stereotype**
U = **Undecided**

_____ 1. All communist nations work together in an attempt to conquer the U.S. and turn the U.S. into a communist state.

_____ 2. Most communist countries are too concerned with internal affairs to consider threatening the U.S.

_____ 3. Any individual in America who favors detente with Russia or China is a communist sympathizer.

_____ 4. Communists are just as concerned and worried as we are about the threat of nuclear war.

_____ 5. All members of the Communist Party of the U.S. believe in the democratic process.

_____ 6. Members of the Communist Party of the U.S. favor the revolutionary overthrow of the present system of government.

_____ 7. All Americans would be better off dead than Red.

_____ 8. The lives of some people living in communist countries have improved since the form of government changed.

_____ 9. All atheists are communists and all communists are atheists.

_____ 10. Communists are just people like us, worried about their families and concerned about their children's future.

_____ 11. Many Americans who were involved in the anti-war movement were communists.

_____ 12. Soldiers in communist countries are better soldiers because they'll do anything they are told to do, just like robots.

BIBLIOGRAPHY

The following list of periodical articles deals with the subject matter of this chapter.

A.S. Abraham — *Limits of Tolerance,* **World Press Review,** November, 1980, p. 41.

R.J. Barnet — *Challenging the Myths of National Security,* **New York Times Magazine,** April 1, 1979, p. 25.

Ezra Taft Benson — *A Moral Challenge to the West,* **Vital Speeches of the Day,** January 15, 1980, p. 198.

R.E. Burns — *Red or Not, Bogeymen Are Just That,* **U.S. Catholic,** May, 1981, p. 2.

Commentary — *Capitalism, Socialism, and Democracy,* April, 1978, p. 29.

Theodore Draper — *Rolling Communism Backward,* **The New Republic,** March 7, 1981, p. 21.

J.J. Guiraldes — *Saving the Western Hemisphere,* **Vital Speeches of the Day,** October 1, 1979, p. 756.

John Judis — *Setting the Stage for Repression,* **The Progressive,** April, 1981, p. 27.

Clare Boothe Luce — *U.S. Foreign Policy and World Communism,* **Vital Speeches of the Day,** August 15, 1978, p. 645

T. Molnar — *Death of Marxist Ideology,* **National Review,** September 14, 1979, p. 1146.

N. Podhoretz — *Future Danger,* **Commentary,** April, 1981, p. 29.

U.S. News & World Report — *Twilight of Communism?,* December 22, 1980, p. 27.

R.G. Wesson — *Marxist Wave Receding,* **USA Today,** December, 1978, p. 5.

T. Yemelyanov — *Hypocrisy of the West,* **Atlas,** March, 1978, p. 44.

Chapter **3**

AMERICAN FOREIGN POLICY

How Should the U.S. Deal With Russia?

"The historic record tells us that the you-can't-trust-the-Russians thesis was deliberately injected into American political consciousness... to win support for a rearmament program."

The Fallacy of a Soviet Threat

Sidney Lens

Sidney Lens is editor of *Liberation* magazine and a contributing editor to *The Progressive.* A former columnist for the *National Catholic Reporter* and former co-chairman of the National Committee to End War in Vietnam, he is current chairman of the Institute for Social Studies. Mr. Lens' publications include *The Military Industrial Complex* (1970) and *The Day before Doomsday* (1977). In the following viewpoint, he claims that the Pentagon has simply used the threat of Russian conquest in order to increase its military appropriations.

Consider the following questions while reading:

1. **How does the author respond to the charge "You can't trust the Russians"?**
2. **What evidence does the author present to support his claim that "the United States, not the Soviet Union, has always taken the initiative in the nuclear arms race"?**
3. **In the author's opinion, how does Washington's approach to national security differ from that of Moscow's?**

Sidney Lens, "But Can We Trust the Russians?," *The Progressive,* July, 1980. Reprinted by permission from *The Progressive,* 409 East Main Street, Madison, Wisconsin 53703. Copyright ©1980, The Progressive, Inc.

You can't trust the Russians.

When budget time rolls around for the Pentagon each year, that five-word sentence constitutes the bottom line — the perennial justification for perpetually increasing military expenditures. Without that basic, unchallenged, and — to most Americans — unchallengeable assumption, the arms race could not go on. Over the past three decades, the United States has spent itself into inflation, economic stagnation, monumental debt, balance-of-payments deficits, a foundering dollar, and lowered living standards — all because of our firm conviction that if anything is certain in this world, it is that you can't trust the Russians.

Well, we *can't* trust the Russians, can we?

We trust the Germans, whom we despised not long ago because they had fought two major wars against the United States. And we trust the Japanese, who perpetrated the "sneak attack" on Pearl Harbor which Franklin D. Roosevelt said would "live in infamy." And we trust the Chinese, who only a few years ago were denounced by us in the same terms we continue to apply to the Soviet Union. Somehow, distrust of the Russians is permanent and irremediable. It is an article of faith for most Americans that if their Government had not spent $2 trillion on its military machine since 1946, the Red Army would now be patrolling Times Square.

The historic record tells us that the you-can't-trust-the-Russians thesis was deliberately injected into American political consciousness after World War II to win support for a rearmament program. Early in the Cold War, President Truman's close collaborator, Republican Senator Arthur Vandenberg, advised the President that if the Government intended to expand military "preparedness," it would have to "scare the hell out of the country." The Soviet "threat" has dominated U.S. policy — and U.S. propaganda — ever since.

YOU CAN'T TRUST ANY GOVERNMENT

But is it really true that you can't trust the Russians — that they are planning and plotting to "take us over"?

To answer the question, you must begin with the fact that you can't trust *any* government. History offers few examples of a regime that would honor its international pledges when those pledges conflict with what it perceives to be "vital interests." The Soviets, who have been preaching the right of peoples to self-determination since Lenin founded the

Bolshevik Party, had no compunction about violating that principle when it seemed that Hungary, Czechoslovakia, and Afghanistan might secede from the Soviet sphere of influence. And the United States has been just as inconsistent in matching promise to performance. Few now remember that Washington promised after World War II that it would never permit Germany to rebuild its military machine, or that it promised permanently to disarm Japan.

PLAYING THE NUMBERS GAME

The army's lobby uses selected numbers to argue that the U.S. has fallen behind the Soviets in military strength.

But the Center for Defense Information has totted up the comparative armed strength, as follows: In Strategic nuclear weapons, the anti-Soviet forces (the U.S., western Europe, and China) have 10,500 nuclear arms; the USSR and its Warsaw Pact allies 6,000. The pro-Soviet forces have 4.8 million men under arms, and its rivals, 9.5 million. The Soviets have 235 major surface ships, the U.S. and its allies 455...

A study of the military budget for the next five years by Employment Research Associates states: "This trillion dollar budget will have a far-reaching and destructive impact on the American economy and society."

There may be fighting, it is true, but in our own cities if inflation grows and funds are taken from social programs.

The Washington Spectator, January 1, 1981.

Nor has our Government adhered to the many agreements, including the United Nations Charter, which prohibit nations from interfering in the internal affairs of others. The CIA engages in such interference every day, overthrowing governments it does not like, and sustaining in power through various means, legal and illegal, the governments it does like. It is inherent in the nature of the nation-state — *any* nation-state — that it seek to retain and expand its influence. One differs from another only in the power at its disposal and the ways it chooses to use that power. You may "trust" a nation when its interests coincide with yours. When they do not, you must find that nation "untrustworthy."

THE U.S. INITIATED NUCLEAR ARMS RACE

In the conflict between the United States and the Soviet Union, therefore, we must ascertain whether, in fact, the Soviets want to "take us over" more than we want to take them over — and what methods each side is prepared to use to achieve its worldwide objectives. We can begin that assessment with the fact that the United States, not the Soviet Union, has always taken the initiative in the nuclear arms race. The United States produced the first atom bomb; the Soviets took four years to catch up. The United States deployed the first hydrogen bomb, the first ballistic missile (despite the Soviets' early space lead), the first nuclear submarine, the first missile with multiple warheads. The United States could have called off the race at any point, and the Soviets would almost certainly have agreed; as the inferior military power, they would have the most to gain from disarmament.

But Washington chose, instead, a course of steady escalation, always hoping to discover an "ultimate" weapon or to gain such overwhelming superiority that the Soviets would be forced to capitulate — to accept U.S. world dominance and dismantle their anti-capitalist system. Though that futile process has brought no political gains to the United States — as even Henry Kissinger has admitted — it continues.

MOSCOW'S DIFFERENT APPROACH

A second point to note is that Moscow and Washington adhere to wholly different approaches to "national security." The Kremlin's principal strategy since 1917 has been to undermine the capitalist system from within.

Vastly outgunned by the capitalist world, the Kremlin put its faith in revolution — national and social — as a means of undermining and dividing its enemies. That policy has worked...

The Soviets suffered reversals here and there, but on the whole they greatly enlarged their influence through non-military means, simply by joining hands with the revolutionaries of Indochina, Angola, Mozambique, Ethiopia, Algeria, Cuba, and other nations. The communist "world" — a single country in 1944 — now encompasses sixteen countries. Even without China and Albania, now hostile to the Soviet

89

"Bring it past the Senate windows; they're discussing the military budget."

Reprinted by permission from the *Daily World*.

Union, the increase in Soviet power and influence is formidable — and so is the decrease in Western power and influence. The Soviets have built an awesome military machine which almost rivals that of the United States, but having achieved such great success by non-military means, they have no need to jeopardize tens of millions of Russian lives by resorting to military means. Soviet leaders are counting on the defeat of capitalism *from within,* not from without. And that is something entirely different from the image conjured up by American leaders, of Soviet troops seizing New York, Chicago, Los Angeles. Understandably, that image "scares the hell" out of many Americans, and makes them willing to accept almost any expenditure that can be rationalized as "defense." But it is no defense against what the Soviets are patiently awaiting: the death of capitalism as a result of its own follies, the triumph of class and national struggles that will demolish the old order.

If that is the Soviet strategy — and history and logic indicate it is — the United States is preparing for the wrong war with the wrong weapons. The notion that you can't trust the Russians becomes totally irrelevant, for what is at issue is not the trust-worthiness of the Soviet Union but the side with which the revolutionary nations of the world choose to align themselves. In that struggle, the American emphasis on militarism is doomed to defeat. The "allies" now sustained by American militarism are, for the most part, anti-revolutionary dictator-ships, and their life span is destined to be relatively brief. And the large sums expended on our military machine cause severe internal problems — debt, deficits, inflation — which erode the true national security of the United States, its econ-omic stability...

The military and their political and corporate allies are caught in a fatal trap: They raise the cry, "You can't trust the Russians," to justify ever larger expenditures for arms; the people and Congress respond by providing the necessary funds for the new weapons; the Soviets reply with counter-weapons of their own, where-upon the military demand new counter-counter-weapons to offset the Soviet "advantage." And in order to get those weapons, they raise the cry, "You can't trust the Russians," all over again. It is a never-ending game.

"The invasion of Afghanistan warns us again of what our future will be if this country does not permanently shed its illusions about the goals of the Soviet dictatorship."

The Soviet Goal of World Conquest

Harry Schwartz

Harry Schwartz is a retired journalist and educator and was formerly on the editorial board of the *New York Times.* A member of the Council on Foreign Relations, his publications include *Prague's 200 Days* (1968) and *The Case for American Medicine* (1972). In the following viewpoint, Mr. Schwartz examines the history of U.S.-Soviet relations and warns that if Soviet aggression goes unchecked, it will culminate in a war involving America.

Consider the following questions while reading:

1. Why does the author claim that we underestimate the Soviet threat?
2. What is the Brezhnev Doctrine?
3. In the author's opinion, how has Vietnam guilt and the lure of profits blurred our vision of true Soviet intentions?

Harry Schwartz, "Lost Illusions," *Newsweek,* January 28, 1980. Reprinted by permission of the author.

It was back in Stalin's time, more than 30 years ago, that Pravda and Isvestia began calling me a "warmonger," "capitalist spy" and similar terms of abuse. My "crime," then and afterward, was writing and publishing articles telling the truth about Stalin's oppressive rule and about the Soviet goal of world conquest. Therefore, it is with a certain wry feeling that I note the chief consequence of the Soviet conquest of Afghanistan: the re-evaluation of Moscow's goals obviously taking place in such different leadership centers as the White House, The New York Times editorial page and the executive offices of Alcoa and other major corporations.

The real surprise to me is not that Moscow did what came naturally to it in Afghanistan, but rather that for long periods many of this country's chief policymakers and opinion-molders deceived themselves about the Soviet Union. At least since Richard M. Nixon and Henry Kissinger announced the wonders of détente in the early 1970s, the American people have been told by their government and by many private-sector leaders that the cold war was essentially over. The Soviet bear, many assured us, had turned into a playful teddy bear with which we could make arms agreements, billion-dollar business deals and cooperative arrangements for scientific research.

A sort of reverse McCarthyism (in the sense of the 1950s) prevailed in this country this past decade. To express doubts about the alleged Soviet transformation, to call attention to Moscow's huge expenditures or rising military strength, to oppose SALT agreements that bound this country more than Moscow, all this was to risk censure even in this land of the free. As I know from personal experience, one was soon called an unthinking cold warrior, a paranoid with a fixation on a non-existent Soviet menace, a hireling of the Pentagon and the arms manufacturers.

THE BREZHNEV DOCTRINE

There was in this country this past decade, it seemed to me, a deliberate effort to obscure many important pages of Soviet history. True, it was Stalin who made Eastern Europe a Soviet satellite, but it was Stalin's successors who used the Red Army against the people of East Berlin in June 1953, against the Hungarians in November 1956, and against the Czechs and Slovaks in August 1968. What Moscow did in Afghanistan was merely to implement the Brezhnev doctrine that Pravda had enunciated in 1968: the principle that the Soviet Union has the obligation to invade and "save" any country that has even a short-lived Communist government in danger of losing power.

How much all of this experience had been forgotten was attested by President Carter's recent almost-unbelievable statement that he had learned more about the Soviet Union in the first week of the conquest of Afghanistan than in all his previous time in the Presidency. Where had Mr. Carter been all these years?

MEETING THE SOVIET CHALLENGE

The greatest problem facing this country today is that of the Soviet Union. Do we, as a people, have the will to meet this challenge? With the Soviets there is no second chance. A society loses its freedom and its values when it fails to understand its own vital processes. Habits of thought, action and attitudes are formulated and accumulated. In the world today, totalitarian ideas sometimes have a greater dynamic than those of the liberal democratic communities. We may not like the options but we are in a global conflict with the Communist nations for survival and decision making on a world basis...Arnold Toynbee puts it this way: "When civilizations fail to meet the challenges of their times, they stagnate, decline, and die."

John D. Garwood, *Vital Speeches of the Day*, May 15, 1980.

The Chinese Communists have shown a much better understanding of the significance of Czechoslovakia in 1968 and a better memory. Both in Mao's last years and since his death, the rulers in Peking have pounded away at Moscow's goal of "hegemony" and warned that that goal threatens all nations, not merely dissidents in the Communist camp. To Peking it must have seemed incredible this past decade that so many political leaders in Washington and Western Europe could have illusions about Moscow and believe seriously that the great conflict of our times had somehow vanished.

Of course, the most sophisticated advocates of détente here always tried to qualify their position. They would mention that the United States and the Soviet Union had opposing interests as well as interests in common. They would suggest that full Washington-Moscow concord was still to be attained. But these and other qualifications tended to be swept away in the tide of détente euphoria that overwhelmed many who should have known better.

Why did so many people in this country who should have known better deceive themselves?

VIETNAM GUILT

One reason, among the intellectuals, was a sense of guilt about Vietnam. Convinced incorrectly that we were the imperialist aggressors in Southeast Asia, many intellectuals — including some key people in the media — in effect rewrote all post-World War II history. To them, the cold war was either a figment of American imagination, or actually the creation of Washington, whose aggressive intentions toward the Soviet Union forced a reluctant and peaceful Stalin, as well as his successors, to arm in self-defense until the United States changed its ways.

THE LURE OF PROFITS

To many businessmen and farmers, acceptance of illusions about the Soviet Union was easy because they were seduced by the thought of huge profits from trade with Moscow and its satellites. There is a strange echo of this thinking in the recent political barrage of denunciations of President Carter for causing losses to farmers by his partial export embargo on grain. From Ted Kennedy to Ronald Reagan, there came seemingly unanimous agreement across the political spectrum that American foreign policy must not cost any farmer even a single dollar. It seemed that none of these would-be presidents understood that if Soviet aggression were allowed to go unchecked and unopposed, it must finally bring an explosion in which American lives would be lost wholesale.

Moreover, it is worth remembering that Moscow has long known how to bribe Americans directly and indirectly to gain its ends. I will never forget a conversation I had with the Soviet ambassador in Washington when Khrushchev visited here in 1959. I started the dialogue by complaining to the ambassador that the Soviet Union would not let me in, and persisted in denying me a visa.

The ambassador assured me that this was a minor hurdle that could be easily surmounted. "All you have to do is write like a progressive journalist," he told me. And when I inquired as to what "progressive journalist" I should take as an example, he said, unperturbed: "Lincoln Steffens," the writer who visited Russia shortly after the Bolshevik Revolution and returned here declaring, "I have seen the future, and it works."

The invasion of Afghanistan warns us again of what our future will be if this country does not permanently shed its illusions about the goals of the Soviet dictatorship. But will this educational experience prove any more enduring than that given by Budapest in 1956 and by Prague in 1968? After all, we no longer have the margin of safety we enjoyed in those earlier times when we were stronger than Moscow, and both of us knew it.

Harry Schwartz

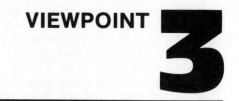

"A foreign policy centered simply on anti-Sovietism makes no sense for the United States."

Anti-Sovietism Makes No Sense

James Chace

James Chace has been managing editor of *Foreign Affairs* magazine since 1970. He has worked on the editorial staffs of *Esquire, East Europe* and *Interplay* and his books include *A World Elsewhere: The New American Foreign Policy* (1973) and *Solvency: The Price of Survival* (1981). In the following viewpoint, Mr. Chace points out that centering foreign policy on anti-Sovietism and attempting to play policeman to the world will cause America to lose the ability to defend its vital interests.

Consider the following questions while reading:

1. Why does the author think that anti-Sovietism may sometimes be counter to American interests?
2. How does the author distinguish between our vital and our general interests?

James Chace, "U.S. Zeros in on the Soviets, Leaving Other Bases Uncovered," *The Minneapolis Star,* May 11, 1981. Reprinted by permission of the author.

A foreign policy centered simply on anti-Sovietism makes no sense for the United States. We have many foreign-policy problems that profoundly affect our vital interests that either do not involve the Soviets directly or invite cooperation with them. An example of the first instance was our debate on turning over jurisdiction of the Panama Canal to the Panamanians — a debate that, stripped of its jingoist overtones, involved questions of America's strategic needs within its traditional sphere of influence, but no Soviet threat to the canal was evident.

ANTI-SOVIETISM AND INTERNATIONAL ORDER

In the second instance, anti-Sovietism is not at the center of such issues as the control of transnational forces that threaten international order — issues such as the environment, exploitation of the seabeds and nuclear proliferation. To deal effectively with these problems requires a recognition that there are overlapping alliances and shifting coalitions — and occasions where the United States and the Soviet Union may have to climb into the same boat or else risk drowning in a sea of problems.

Although not every Soviet move is directed against us, the threat of Soviet expansionism is not something that we should ever remain indifferent to. For example, Soviet support of Vietnam is primarily aimed at the containment of China — but there is always the danger that Vietnam, a Soviet ally, after expanding into Cambodia, might thrust into Thailand, whose government is aligned with ours. At that point, we should have to decide on the nature of our support for Thailand — do we provide military aid in dollars only or military advisers or actual troops on the ground? To answer these questions, we would also have to determine the degree of our commitment, given our finite resources, to confront the Soviets in areas of marginal interest.

To advance our foreign-policy goals involves not only devising military and diplomatic strategies to contend with the growing trend of a Soviet Union that seems bent on increasing its power and influence in the Third World, but also using our economic power to influence the behavior of other nations that may or may not be the objects of Soviet foreign policy. Yet our aid to less developed nations is decreasing. It fell by 38 percent between 1961 and 1977.

Moreover, we have concentrated our limited resources on two Middle Eastern countries, Israel and Egypt, which received 80 percent of total U.S. military assistance in 1979.

James Chace

Even though, after the fall of Gen. Anastasio Somoza, many in Congress feared that Nicaragua would become "another Cuba" — that is, a Soviet ally dependent on aid from Havana and Moscow — Congress itself delayed for almost a year approving and releasing a paltry $75 million in supplementary aid to the struggling new government.

While U.S. assistance programs cannot ensure political leverage over others, they can at least force the recipients to take account of America's interests and the incentives that such aid provides. If we continue cutting back on aid and trade concessions as inducements to political cooperation while spending vast sums on new weaponry, we simply deprive ourselves of valuable assets that we should be using to advance our foreign-policy interests.

BUILDING BOMBS FOR THE WRONG WAR

The more of our energy and resources we squander on preparation for the wrong war, the closer we come to the collapse anticipated by the Soviets. Our true enemy today is not communism or Soviet ambition but world hunger. Some 2.5 billion human beings live on an average income of $4.50 a week; a half billion are utterly destitute; more than a billion lack access to clean water. So long as the American Establishment insists on responding to that crisis by building more bombs, it drives the desperate people of the world into the arms of its adversary.

Sidney Lens and George Ott, *The Progressive*, October, 1979.

VITAL AND GENERAL INTERESTS

Our need in foreign policy, as in domestic policy, is to act in accordance with our means, distinguishing our vital from our general interests. But we must be clear in our own minds what these interests are. The geographical position of the United States is such that it should be able to protect itself in its own hemisphere without threatening the independence of others. Western Europe, Japan and, for many special reasons, Israel remain vital to American interests, not only because we share moral and political values but also because we have strong economic ties with them. We always have correctly believed that any Soviet expansion into these areas would be a direct threat to us. Though the Third World beyond the Western Hemisphere remains an area of serious American interest, it becomes a vital interest only insofar as we, or our allies, remain gravely dependent on foreign natural resources. By this definition, the Persian Gulf is a vital interest.

Far from defining the vital interests outside the Western Hemisphere as the maintenance of our alliances with Western Europe and Japan — to say nothing of trying to ensure a continuing supply of oil from the Persian Gulf — President Reagan's foreign policy and defense task force concluded that "no area of the world is beyond the scope of American interests" and that the United States would need to have "sufficient military standing to cope with any level of violence" around the globe. In a world where America plays policeman, the distinction between our vital and our secondary interests inevitably blurs, and in an effort to impose a Pax Americana, we will even risk losing our ability to defend ourselves beyond the Western Hemisphere itself.

Anti-Sovietism is at once too much and not enough to constitute the essence of American foreign policy. What we need is a policy that opposes the Soviet Union only at points where we have the resources to oppose the Soviets successfully. But beyond that, we need a positive policy that affirmatively advances U.S. interests even when the Soviet Union is not involved.

"In the past ten years there has been a decided shift in the balance of military power from the U.S. to the Soviet Union."

Defending Against Soviet Expansionism

Strom Thurmond

Strom Thurmond has been a U.S. Senator from South Carolina since 1955. A 1948 presidential candidate for the State's Rights Party, he was a teacher, lawyer and governor of South Carolina before entering the Senate. In the following viewpoint, Thurmond discusses national defense, emphasizing the shifting balance of power in favor of Russia, and warns that only the U.S. can end the spiral into world disorder by resuming a position of leadership in the free world.

Consider the following questions while reading:

1. What evidence does the author present in claiming the Soviet Union is a threat to the United States?
2. What does the author say about our present defense position?

Strom Thurmond, "Defense for America," *Vital Speeches of the Day*, October 15, 1980. Reprinted by permission.

The founders of our nation set forth as one of the primary goals of our Federal government the preservation of our national security. Unfortunately, the percent of our Federal budget which has gone to defense in recent years amounts to about 23 percent, the lowest level since World War II. While we have lagged in defense spending, the Soviet Union has greatly accelerated their effort and are currently outspending the U.S. by at least 40 percent annually.

These trends in defense, the U.S. decline and the Soviet buildup, have become in the past several years a major political issue...

I do not believe a nuclear exchange or a head-on conflict with the Soviet Union is likely. The greater threat we face is that the Soviets will use their military power to expand their sphere of influence by denying us the support of our allies and denying us the free flow of raw materials we need for our industrial and defense growth, including the petroleum needed to run our economy.

FOUR SUBJECTS

My purpose this morning will be to comment briefly on four issues...

The four subjects I would like to comment on are as follows:

First, *the shifting balance of power;* Second, *our defense position today;* Third, *the transfer of Western technology to Communist nations,* and Fourth, *Soviet Expansionism.*

THE SHIFTING BALANCE OF POWER

In the past ten years there has been a decided shift in the balance of military power from the U.S. to the Soviet Union. After the U.S. withdrawal from Vietnam, defense spending fell drastically, as a general "reordering of priorities" took place.

These trends can be illustrated quite dramatically in the area of strategic military strength. In 1969 the U.S. led the Soviet Union in nearly every measure of defense systems: the numbers of land and sea-based missiles, the accuracy of these weapons, the numbers of warheads, and the megatonnage of our missile forces.

Now, ten years later after implementing SALT I and negotiating a follow-on SALT II Treaty, we find the Soviets have equalled or lead the U.S. in all of these categories except the number of warheads. In this final category, our defense leaders report the Soviets will be superior by 1985.

Our leaders, especially in the last few years, have promoted

Strom Thurmond

a policy of military parity with the Soviets, but while we engaged in unilateral arms restraint, the Soviets conducted a massive buildup of their strategic nuclear weapons, their Navy and their conventional forces...

It is now clear to most qualified observers that the Soviets are not interested in a position of parity, but seek a *clear military superiority.* This shift is even better perceived overseas than here in the U.S. Recently, the former Prime Minister of Great Britain, Harold MacMillan, summed up the feelings of many when he stated, "Things are as bad for the West as they could possibly be and they are getting worse."

In my opinion, this shifting balance of power is extremely dangerous. This Soviet buildup is far in excess of any defensive needs.

OUR DEFENSE POSITION TODAY

With this background on the shift of military power over the past ten years and mounting evidence of Soviet use of this power, such as in Afghanistan, I would like to now address my second point, *our defense position today.*

In Senate testimony this year, our military leaders have admitted that the U.S. has lost strategic nuclear superiority to the Soviets. This situation cannot be reversed until the late 1980s, even if we accelerate various strategic programs now in development.

This situation came about because of our idealistic foreign policies of the past ten years, our continued inability to understand the Soviet threat and our failure to go forward with defense programs to assure — without a doubt — our military strength will be second to none.

For instance, our strategic strength was endangered by the cancellation of the B-1 bomber. Pilots today are flying the old B-52, a bomber older than some of the pilots. It represents technology of the 1950s, yet the Administration plans to use it into the 1990s.

In the area of land-based missiles, called ICBMs, the Administration has delayed the new mobile MX missile to the point that it will be 1987 before the first units can be operational. This delay took place despite the fact that improved accuracy in new Soviet missiles will enable them to destroy 90% of our Minuteman force in a first strike in the early 1980s.

Navy Below Strength: Besides our problems in long range strategic weapons, we have allowed the numbers of ships in our Navy to fall well below that needed for protecting the sea lanes over which our exports and imports flow. The Chief of Naval Operations, Admiral Thomas Hayward, has testified that we are "trying to meet a three-ocean requirement with a one and one-half ocean Navy."

In the area of conventional equipment, the story is unfortunately much the same — we are behind and falling even further behind. The Soviets lead the U.S. in *tanks and armored personnel carriers, 4 to 1;* in *artillery pieces, 8 to 1;* and in *helicopters and tactical aircraft, 2 to 1.*

AN AGGRESSIVE ADVERSARY

To frustrate Soviet global strategy, it is necessary, first and foremost, to acknowledge that it exists. We must get rid of the notion, widespread among America's educated and affluent, that the Soviet Union acts out of fear, that its actions are invariably reactions to U.S. initiatives, and that it seizes targets of opportunity like some kind of international pickpocket. We are dealing with an adversary who is driven not by fear but by aggressive impulses, who is generally more innovative in the field of political strategy than we are, and who selects his victims carefully, with long-term objectives in mind.

Richard Pipes, *Commentary*, April, 1980.

Other major problems facing the military services are the lack of sufficient numbers of missiles and spare parts to keep our planes and equipment operating. For instance, we are paying $15 million for F-14 aircraft, yet each plane has only 2 Phoenix missiles to use in wartime. We have spent $500 million to buy attack submarines, yet the numbers of torpedoes are not sufficient to allow two loads per submarine.

Personnel Shortages: Another issue of great importance is the failure of the all-volunteer force to attract the quantity and quality of personnel to operate our military units. We have spent billions on the all-volunteer force, but if it fails, we must return to the draft...

TRANSFER OF WESTERN TECHNOLOGY

Moving now to my third point, I would like to comment briefly on the transfer of high technology to the Soviets through ill-advised trade policies.

Unfortunately, the United States has sold many high technology items which our enemies have used to their advantage. Trucks built with American technology at the Soviet Kama River truck plant were used in the invasion of Afghanistan.

Computers have been exported which have found use in factories that produce missile launchers. Wide body jet technology sold for commercial use has found its way into military aircraft. Ball bearing technology we have sold to the Soviets is being used to improve the accuracy of Soviet strategic missiles. This improved accuracy of Soviet missiles now threatens our own Minuteman ICBM system.

We are continuing to sell items to the Soviets — items such as nuclear reactor parts, transistors, test instrumentation, and advanced oil drilling materials, all of which have military as well as commercial applications. Dr. William J. Perry, Undersecretary of Defense for Research and Engineering, in testifying this year to the Senate Armed Services Committe on this subject stated that "I think we made some errors in judgment."

U.S. Finances Soviet Purchases: Another shocking dimension to this trade policy is the fact that the U.S. has financed the sale of some of these high technology items to the Soviets. From 1972 to 1975, during the height of the detente policy, we permitted the Soviet Union to draw official Export-Import Bank credits, guaranteed by the United States Government, at very favorable low interest rates. Now, five years after Congress put a stop to this practice, the Soviet Union still owes us approximately $447 million for these credits.

In addition to these official credits, the Soviet Union owes U.S. commercial banks about $815 million. The adverse effect of these loans is twofold. First, we are financing a nation which is creating problems for us throughout the world; and second, certain U.S. interests lobby for an unrealistic policy with the Soviets in order not to endanger the repayment of these loans...

RIP VAN UNCLE

SOVIET INTENTIONS

U.S. DEFENSE

SOVIET EXPANSIONISM

It is against this background that I would like to talk briefly about my fourth point, *Soviet expansionism.*

Although Soviet military strength compared to the U.S. in the 1970s was marginal, they continued their expansionist policies and with a great deal of success. For instance, their support of North Vietnam has now lead to the Communist takeover of South Vietnam, Cambodia and Laos in Indochina. The threat to Thailand and other nations of this area merely awaits the resolution of whether the pro-Chinese or pro-Soviet forces will prevail in Cambodia.

In Africa, they have used Cuban proxy troops and Russian-built military equipment to bring pro-Soviet forces to power in Angola, Mozambique and Ethiopia. Cuban forces have also been introduced into the Middle East in South Yemen, and last December Soviet troops were used for the first time in recent years when the invasion of Afghanistan was launched. Today the people of Afghanistan are being brutalized daily by the raw power of Soviet helicopters, tanks and guns which have destroyed entire villages to secure the Soviet puppet leader's control. Even Afghan military units have been destroyed when they attempted to revolt.

Closer to home, the Soviets have established air and naval bases in Cuba, conducted maneuvers with a sizable military unit there and aided Cuba in its export of revolution throughout Latin America. Nicaragua has fallen to Marxist forces, aided by Cuba and Panama; and now El Salvador and other nations are threatened...

CONCLUSIONS

Thus, the question arises — if Soviet expansionism makes such gains during a period of relative parity, what will happen in the 1980s during a period of Soviet military dominance? The answer to that question might still be subject to our control if we turn our shoulder to the wheel and restore our military strength.

This spiral into world disorder must be ended if your generation and future generations are to enjoy periods of relative peace. This can only be accomplished by the U.S. asserting itself again, resuming its position as leader of the Free World, aiding our allies who face Communist aggression and maintaining our own military strength...

Finally, I would like to note that we would be well served to refer back to the greatest book ever written for advise in these perilous times. First, in the Book of Proverbs, we find this admonition — "where there is no vision, the people perish;" and second, in Luke, "when a strong man armed keepeth his place, his goods are in peace."

"The United States must project itself to the Third World as a revolutionary system which has brought prosperity to the American working class... and...expose false USSR propaganda concerning America and tell the truth about Soviet colonialism in Central Asia and Eastern Europe."

How to Deal with Russia

Richard F. Staar

Richard F. Staar has been associate director of the Hoover Institute on War, Revolution and Peace at Stanford University since 1969. He is the author of *Poland 1944-62: The Sovietization of a Captive People* (revised, 1975) and *Communist Regimes in Eastern Europe* (revised, 1977). In the following viewpoint, Mr. Staar offers suggestions for a course of action to counter Soviet propaganda, espionage and efforts to gain control of Third World countries.

Consider the following questions while reading:

1. What examples of Soviet hostility does the author cite in the following areas: propaganda, information gathering, foreign trade, and military strength?
2. What five United States policy responses does the author recommend?

Richard F. Staar, "United States Relations With the USSR," *Vital Speeches of the Day*, July 15, 1980. Reprinted by permission.

One often assumes that others have motives similar to our own. Such "mirror imaging" can be dangerous, however, when applied to Soviet leaders whose world outlook has been formed under completely different conditions. Most of them never received a secondary education, having been selected for technical or political training at the college level with only an elementary school background. That may explain why many are only semi-educated, in the conventional sense of the word.

The new Soviet leadership during the 1980s will be faced with many problems: economic, structural and cultural, as well as others...

SOVIET PROPAGANDA

Foreign Propaganda. Despite difficulties of a domestic or intra-Bloc nature, the Soviet propaganda machine almost certainly will continue its campaign of glorifying alleged USSR achievements while at the same time denigrating the West in general and the United States in particular...

Apart from fronts and conferences at the élite level, Soviet foreign propaganda attacking the United States floods the world via radio. During 1980, the USSR will devote some 2,000 hours per week to broadcasting in 83 foreign languages over Radio Moscow alone...

INFORMATION GATHERING

Information gathering involves professionals, frequently utilizing journalism as a cover, and hence propaganda activities overlap with espionage. Hundreds of Soviet newsmen assigned to foreign posts are in reality intelligence officers who report directly to their own headquarters in Moscow. In addition, it is estimated that at least half of all Bloc officials abroad work either for the KGB or GRU, civilian military intelligence agencies, respectively. To the more than 3,000 Soviets and East Europeans (i.e., about 1,500 spies) attached to embassies in Washington, D.C., and consulates or the U.N. in New York must be added those wives who also work as agents. That does not include 65,000 visitors to the United States each year from the Bloc, some of whom will certainly have intelligence assignments.

The United States, one of the most open societies in the world, also is the target of a massive effort at Soviet industrial espionage...

111

FOREIGN TRADE

Foreign trade always has been looked upon by Soviet leaders as an instrument of economic warfare. The USSR and its East European client states as of 1980 owe the industrialized West more than sixty billion dollars in long and short-term credits which have been borrowed to finance imports. An important question is whether such an acceleration of loans is in the national interest of non-communist Western countries, because these huge debts make economic hostages of business firms as well as official and quasi-official lending agencies...

It should be mentioned also that several thousand graduate students from the USSR and Eastern Europe have received technical training in the United States.

IDEOLOGICAL WARFARE

For the first time in the American experience we must learn how to employ ideological warfare in the national defense. Thus we must study our enemy and his tactics which have been so successful in many parts of the world that we might profit by his experience and our ignorance or aloofness of the past. People are won not by money but by ideology, yet our liberal foreign policy shapers have never been able to come to grips with this cold-blooded reality.

Unless we can convince people — through propaganda — that they should follow and support American leadership, as opposed to Communist or "Socialist" seduction, we might as well keep our AID money home for better purposes.

Bill Miller, *Manchester Union Leader*, July 23, 1980.

Brezhnev explained the rationale behind the foregoing in a secret briefing to East European leaders at the height of détente. An excerpt from the speech was reported on 17 September, 1973 by the *New York Times* as follows:

"To the Soviet Union, the policy of accommodation does

112

represent a tactical policy shift over the next 15 or so years. The Soviet Union intends to pursue accords with the West and at the same time build up its own economic and military strength.

At the end of this period, in the middle 1980s, the strength of the Soviet Union will have increased to the point at which we, instead of relying on accords, could establish an independent, superior position in dealing with the West"...

MILITARY STRENGTH

Military strength and the rapid build-up of armed forces, as well as projection of power also via surrogates, have played an important role in USSR relations with the United States. Over the past decade, measured in constant dollars, Soviet military expenditures have exceeded American spending by $150 billion. The CIA prediction is that this long-range growth trend will continue into the 1980s...

USSR leaders fully comprehend the destructiveness of nuclear war. That is why they continue demanding of their people the sacrifices required to expand military power and fund a civil defense program ten times that of the United States. Does this mean that the Soviets will attack when they have achieved a "correlation of forces" to their advantage? Probably not. However, they do realize that overwhelming superiority will allow them to blackmail the West, obtain their objectives without bloodshed, and in this manner avoid a mutually destructive nuclear exchange.

THE U.S. RESPONSE

Policy recommendations in Washington should be predicated upon a clear understanding that future Soviet leaders will continue to differ in both outlook and attitude from their American counterparts. Subterfuge, dissembling, and outright dishonesty cannot be explained away in terms of USSR suspicions of fear of U.S. strategic power which, in actual fact, has been on the decline since 1956 when President Eisenhower refused to support Britain and France during the Suez crisis and has continued to deteriorate during subsequent administrations. The following are suggested as possible courses for action:

(1) Without waiting for a change that cannot possibly occur in the USSR unless incentive exists, Washington should establish a small group of experts to analyze USSR propaganda activities, not only to monitor Russian language publications and broadcasts over Radio Moscow as well as over

Radio Peace and Progress but systematically and persistently to refute them. The anti-American propaganda campaign has continued, despite détente. Exposing its themes by the Voice of America and Radio Free Europe/Radio Liberty would soon disabuse the Kremlin of the idea that it can continue the same "cold war" approach toward audiences inside the USSR and throughout the Third World via international front organizations, without any response or retaliation.

(2) Espionage capability can be reduced by limiting the Soviet embassy and consulates in the United States to the

Richard F. Staar

same number of American diplomatic personnel assigned to the USSR. If one of its citizens is caught involved with activities incompatible with his or her status, reciprocal expulsion should not be accepted and no replacement allowed to enter this country. That was exactly what Britain did when it declared 105 Soviet officials personae non grata, comprising one-fifth of all such persons in London. The same thing occurred in Canada on a more limited basis only last year. The USSR did not retaliate in either case, when warned of reciprocal treatment.

(3) Foreign trade with the USSR, which imported about $8.5 billion worth of goods more than it exported to the United States during six years of "détente" and accumulated a huge debt, has not led to improved relations. Helping Moscow solve its economic difficulties by shipments of grain and advanced technology continued to be counterproductive. The United States would strengthen its position by requiring the Soviet Union periodically to balance its account and make up the deficit by supplying this country with petroleum and other raw materials which are needed here.

(4) If an American citizen is roughed up, interrogated by the secret police, and convicted on the basis of falsified evidence, the USSR ambassador to Washington should be told in no uncertain terms that he will be expelled and/or his counterpart in Moscow recalled, if such harassment is not stopped immediately. Accreditation of Soviet journalists should be revoked when their counterparts are harassed by agent-provocateurs as happened on several occasions in Moscow and Tashkent during the past year.

(5) The United States must project itself to the Third World as a revolutionary system which has brought prosperity to the American working class, where skilled laborers sometimes earn more money then professors, and where human rights are practiced rather than preached. The corollary would be a campaign that will expose false USSR propaganda concerning America and tell the truth about Soviet colonialism in Central Asia and Eastern Europe.

Finally, the Soviet Union suffers from multiple contradictions: between Russians and other nationalities, party élite and masses, the USSR and its dependencies in Eastern Europe. Why is it that spokesmen for the United States never criticize the fraudulent march toward a "classless" society or the virulent atheism which persecutes Christianity, Islam, and Judaism? It should be pointed out that the American political system enables both groups and individuals to associate freely. They are allowed to propose policies and programs that are at variance with U.S. Government policy. This is the essence of the free way of life and must be projected forcefully on the international scene.

DISTINGUISHING PRIMARY FROM SECONDARY SOURCES

A critical thinker must always question his or her sources of knowledge. One way to critically evaluate information is to be able to distinguish between PRIMARY SOURCES (a "firsthand" or eyewitness account from personal letters, documents, or speeches, etc.) and SECONDARY SOURCES (a "secondhand" account usually based upon a "firsthand" account and possibly appearing in newspapers, encyclopedias, or other similar types of publications). A diary about the Civil War written by a Civil War veteran is an example of a primary source. A history of the Civil War written many years after the war and relying, in part, upon that diary for information is an example of a secondary source. However, it must be noted that interpretation and/or point of view also play a role when dealing with primary and secondary sources. For example, the historian writing about the Civil War not only will quote from the veteran's diary but also will interpret it. That his or her interpretation may be incorrect is certainly a possibility. Even the diary or primary source must be questioned as to interpretation and point of view. The veteran may have been a militarist who stressed the glory of warfare rather than the human suffering involved.

Test your skill in evaluating sources by participating in the following exercise. Pretend that your teacher has asked you to write a research paper on the history of U.S. - Russian relations. You are also asked to distinguish the primary sources you used from the secondary sources. Listed below are ten sources which may be useful in your research. Carefully evaluate each of them. First, place a P next to those descriptions you feel would serve as primary sources. Second, rank the primary sources assigning the number (1) to the most

objective and accurate primary source, number (2) to the next accurate and so on until the ranking is finished. Repeat the entire procedure, this time placing an S next to those descriptions you feel would serve as secondary sources and then ranking them. Discuss and compare your evaluations with other class members.

P or S   **Rank In Importance**

_____ 1. A history of World War II written by a   _____
             Russian historian.

_____ 2. An autobiography written by Joseph   _____
             Stalin.

_____ 3. A book on the Cuban missile crisis   _____
             written by Robert F. Kennedy.

_____ 4. An editorial in a Russian magazine   _____
             defending Russia's right to place
             missiles in Cuba.

_____ 5. A NATO general testifying befóre the   _____
             Senate Defense Committe budget
             hearings.

_____ 6. An article in _Time_ magazine reporting   _____
             on the Senate Defense Committee
             budget hearings.

_____ 7. The U.S. representative to the SALT II   _____
             negotiations reporting to a joint
             session of Congress.

_____ 8. The 1968 _Pravda_ (Russian newspaper)   _____
             article outlining the Brezhnev
             doctrine.

_____ 9. A 1968 feature in _The New York Times_   _____
             analyzing the Brezhnev doctrine as
             outlined in _Pravda._

_____ 10. A research paper published by the   _____
             Foundation for Foreign Affairs out-
             lining the historical impact of the cold
             war years.

BIBLIOGRAPHY

The following list of periodical articles deals with the subject matter of this chapter.

Richard Barnet — *Lies Clearer Than Truth,* **Sojourners,** August, 1979, p. 16.

Bruce Bartlett — *De-Mythologizing the Soviet Menace,* **The Libertarian Review.** April, 1980, p. 32.

Ralph Kinney Bennett — *Soviet Military Might: Made in U.S.A.,* **The Reader's Digest.** August, 1980, p. 75.

Christianity and Crisis — *The U.S. and the U.S.S.R: War or Peace?,* May 26, 1980, entire issue.

Miles Copeland — *Why the Soviets Aren't Worried,* **National Review,** January 4, 1980, p. 24.

John P. East — *Does the USSR Really Support International Terrorism?,* **Human Events,** June 13, 1981, p. 12.

John D. Garwood — *The Soviet Threat: Our Greatest Problem,* **Vital Speeches of the Day,** May 15, 1980, p. 458.

Sanford Gottlieb — *Russia's Weaknesses,* **Newsweek,** March 26, 1979, p. 19.

Sidney Lens and George Ott — *The Wrong Debate: America is Losing the Real War,* **The Progressive,** October, 1979, p. 14.

John Lukacs — *The Light in the East,* **The New Republic,** September 20, 1980, p. 17.

Robert Moss — *What Russia Wants,* **The New Republic,** January 19, 1980, p. 23.

Victor Perlo — *The Myth of Soviet Superiority,* **The Nation,** September 13, 1980, p. 1.

Richard Pipes — *Soviet Global Strategy,* **Commentary,** April, 1980, p. 31.

U.S. News & World Report — *View From Moscow: A World More Dangerous Than Ever,* January 19, 1981, p. 35.

George F. Will — *Wishing Away the Soviet Threat,* **Conservative Digest,** April, 1979, p. 34.

Chapter

How Should the U.S. Deal With Third World Countries?

"Americans cherish the belief that they export their democratic values and prevent the spread of dictatorships throughout the world. This, unfortunately, is simply not true."

The Arrogance of American Policy

M.J. Akbar

This critical look at American foreign policy is authored by M.J. Akbar, the editor of *Sunday,* a leading weekly news journal published in India. In the following viewpoint, Mr. Akbar claims that American policy, particularly toward Third World countries, is not as idealistic as claimed. Indeed, he assails American arrogance and states that the real objective of American foreign policy is to prevent dictatorships *only* when they challenge American interests.

Consider the following questions while reading:

1. **How does the author claim that American foreign policy is like Russian foreign policy?**
2. **Why does the author support the price raises of OPEC nations?**
3. **What example of American lack of respect for African nations does the author cite?**

M.J. Akbar, "Arrogant America," *The Nation,* September 13, 1980. Copyright 1980 The Nation Associates.

Americans like to believe that their foreign policy has been grounded in ideology: that they protect and support something called the Free World against something perfectly ghastly called Communism. This belief originates in part from the kind of society that the Americans have created for themselves — by and large a free society.

DICTATORS & AMERICAN INTERESTS

Americans cherish the belief that they export their democratic values and prevent the spread of dictatorships throughout the world. This, unfortunately, is simply not true. The real objective of American policy is to prevent the spread of dictatorships that challenge American interests. Otherwise, it is very comfortable with dictatorship indeed. A rough count of the number of baton-waving generals or robber-kings whom the Americans have supported and continue to support belies the United States' pretensions of international morality. And in case anyone felt that there was some degree of consistency in that at least the United States was supporting anti-Communist governments, Richard Nixon demonstrated (with the support of the American electorate) that the United States could willingly help a left-wing dictatorship if it was in its interests to do so — thus, the "successful" China policy. Indeed, America finds its greatest difficulty in getting along with democracies like India, which feel that they must think for themselves.

THE ARROGANCE OF AMERICAN POLICY

American foreign policy, like Russian foreign policy toward its satellite states, is rooted in arrogance. This is the arrogance that says that while the rest of the world must understand the United States and its needs, the United States has no obligation to understand other nations (e.g., Iran and its revolution) if it does not wish to. Such arrogance holds that other nations do not necessarily need democracy and freedom; what they need are governments that have Washington's blessing. No matter that such governments are headed by barbarous, sadistic and inhuman robbers like the Shah of Iran or the feudal monarchs of Saudi Arabia.

This same arrogance makes America believe that its citizens have some divine right to pay less than half as much for gasoline as the rest of the world does. Why should U.S. drivers pay less? Why shouldn't the Organization of Petroleum Exporting Countries raise its prices, and why does each price rise create such an outcry? After all, OPEC is only finally and very belatedly doing what Adam Smith told capitalists to do a long while ago. Americans react to decisions made by other nations in such a frenzy because they have never tried to understand any viewpoint other than their own. And because they have convinced themselves that what they stand for is Right and Justice, they feel that anyone who disagrees with them is on the side of Evil.

The United States has always defined its enemy very simply; the Enemy is anyone who attacks U.S. interests. Nothing else matters. Friends are constantly being kissed on both cheeks — like President Mohammad Zia ul-Haq of Pakistan, who surprised everyone when he got upset at being so effusively kissed. The United States is always on the lookout for only one thing: friends who will listen more frequently to Washington than to their own people. There are certainly no principles involved. And thus the United States continues to confuse power with stability: President Zia may be powerful today, but his Government is certainly not stable, and the strong opposition

WHAT THE THIRD WORLD BELIEVES

Much of the Third World believes that U.S. foreign policy seeks repressive stability in regimes round the world so that American business can accumulate maximum profit. Even U.S. foreign aid is taken not as charity but as a kind of reparations fund for offenses past and future. Aside from the usual resentment human nature feels at another's generosity, there is a Third World conviction that the U.S. is impurely promoting its own interests with aid. Few in the Third World believe that the U.S. values humanity more than money.

Lance Morrow, *Time*, January 14, 1980.

to him in Pakistan cannot possibly approve of U.S. aid that would only prop him up in power a little longer and do very little indeed to drive the Russians out of Afghanistan. This search for friends irrespective of their intrinsic worth, their present or potential value, is what is increasingly leading the United States into all sorts of trouble in a fast-changing world.

AMERICA & THE THIRD WORLD

Nobody in the Third World, including India, which Americans suspect is a Russian surrogate only because it refuses to be a United States surrogate, likes the idea of a Russian bear hug. What happened in Afghanistan, in any case, was not a bear hug, but simple rape. But if nobody likes Russian soldiers, nobody likes the idea of the *U.S.S. Enterprise* patrolling nearby waters either. Almost all the Third World nations have come to realize that the way to fight one superpower is not by jumping into the arms of another. The world is not ringing up Big Brother anymore (mainly because Big Brothers tend to confuse affection and rape); the nations of the Third World are ringing one another up. Why? Because Small Brother is not so small anymore; Small Brother has grown up.

Small Brothers know that the ability of both the United States and Russia to insult them is undiminished. While the Soviet Union of course has given us the classic example in Afghanistan, the United States in its own way showed how much respect it had for the black nations of Africa — in a much less harmful way, to be sure, and one that was regarded by the United States as a friendly gesture. I refer to the decision to send former heavyweight champion Muhammad Ali to Africa to persuade black nations to boycott the Olympics. Ali may be a great boxer, but is he the man to send on a sensitive diplomatic mission? France sent a team to the Moscow Olympics. Would President Carter send Jimmy Connors, or better still, Chris Evert Lloyd in her shorts, to persuade President Valéry Giscard d'Estaing to change his mind? No. D'Estaing is a white head of state, you see. He is a sensible man. Carter's Georgian Mafia remains precisely that — Georgian.

The United States is going through a period when the Lying Adjective and the Angry Hyperbole have taken over its thought processes. These are perilous times.

"Nations like Tanzania and Venezuela are not impoverished because of Northern Hemisphere affluence but because of their own internal inefficiencies and corruption."

Third World Poverty Is Not Our Fault

Andrew M. Greeley

Sociologist, writer and Roman Catholic priest, Andrew Greeley is one of America's most widely read editorialists. He has been Director of the Center for Study of American Pluralism since 1973 and Professor of Sociology at the University of Arizona since 1978. Father Greeley's books include *Death and Beyond* (1976) and *The Magic Cup: An Irish Legend* (1979). In the following viewpoint, he examines two Third World nations which have received billions in foreign aid and claims that their disastrous economic plight cannot be blamed on the affluent nations of the world.

Consider the following questions while reading:
1. **What examples of Tanzanian inefficiencies does the author cite?**
2. **What examples of Venezuelan inefficiencies does the author cite?**
3. **Do you agree with the author's conclusion?**

Andrew M. Greeley, "Third World Poverty is Not Our Fault," *Human Events,* May 12, 1979. Reprinted by permission of Universal Press Syndicate.

The Third World, we are told, is poor because the rest of us are rich.

Let us look at two rather special Third World countries, Tanzania and Venezuela. The former country is noteworthy because it has a Christian Socialist (indeed, Roman Catholic) president and because the Northern Hemisphere has poured billions of dollars into it in the last 17 years. Venezuela is noteworthy because it is one of the few countries in the Third World that has political democracy; indeed, in a free election recently it changed ruling parties.

They are also interesting examples because Tanzania is a very poor country and Venezuela is a very rich one (because of its oil exports). The latter has received billions of dollars in oil payments and the former billions of dollars in grants from "Northern" nations.

TANZANIA

Both are economic disasters. Julius Nyerere, the idealistic dictator of Tanzania, was convinced that socialized collective farming and "barefoot socialism" would transform one of the world's poorest nations. Ninety-five percent of the population has moved into collective farming villages — a forced ruralization of the economy. Not everybody was enthused by the *"ujamaa"* approach, as this collectivization was called. When necessary, they were persuaded to cooperate at gunpoint.

Despite his visionary idealism, Nyerere had not apparently read about the failure of collectivized farming in other countries. The health clinics, schools and agricultural development aid that were supposed to materialize after collectivization simply did not appear. Low incentives did not challenge idealism — they never do — but only guaranteed even more inefficient management. Per capita income is $198 per year. There are almost no foreign exchange reserves. Tanzania is in worse internal and external economic shape than it was when Nyerere came to power.

In other words, the ideological mistake of Tanzanian leadership caused that nation to waste the billions of dollars of foreign aid that was poured into it. Despite all the money, 17 years later Tanzania is as desperately impoverished a place as it ever was.

VENEZUELA

Venezuela gets lots of foreign money, too: $11 billion a year in petroleum income. It has freeways and highrises and luxury imports which grow at the annual rate of 30 percent. But despite the billions of dollars it more or less extorts from the rest of the world, 40 percent of Venezuela's 13 million people live in abject poverty. One out of three lives in a slum; the slums are growing. A million children are abandoned every year and 10 percent of the children born in the country suffer physical or mental defects. Its unemployment rate is 25 percent. Its inflation is astronomical. The government and ruling classes are permeated with corruption.

Official aid goes to governments, not to poor people. Its expenditure is governed by the personal and professional ambitions of politicians and civil servants. Much is spent on politically inspired prestige projects: airlines, inefficient industries...and construction of new capitals at vast cost (Brasilia, Islamabad, Dodoma in Tanzania)...

The Western democracies became industrial societies without foreign aid, argues Dr. Peter Bauer; and those nations of Asia, Africa and Latin America, where economic progress is greatest — Taiwan, South Korea, Singapore, Malaysia, Kenya, the Ivory Coast, Brazil — are also those least dependent on economic assistance.

Patrick Buchanan, *Los Angeles Herald Examiner*, February 19, 1980.

Still the Venezuelan government is able to afford an expensive public relations campaign. A couple of years ago I wrote a column critical of the government of the country and promptly got on the mailing list for its American image-makers. If you can't do anything about poverty, at least you can try to change the image of poverty...

Venezuela, then, is a Third World country which has more money than it knows what to do with, the result of a superabundance (temporary) in natural resources. The result is more poverty, inflation and unemployment. Tanzania is a poor Third World country because it lacks natural resources. Both have received enormous contributions from the Northern Hemisphere: voluntary contributions in the case of Tanzania, compulsory in the case of Venezuela. Both have squandered the money they have received. In both, the condition of the poor people is worse than ever before.

CONCLUSION

When the theorists, the ideologues and the liberation theologians are finally willing to face the harsh reality that nations like Tanzania and Venezuela are not impoverished because of Northern Hemisphere affluence but because of their own internal inefficiencies and corruption, then perhaps poverty in the Third World will begin to decline.

"El Salvador has been progressively transformed into another case of indirect armed aggression against a small Third World country by Communist powers acting through Cuba."

Communist Aggression in El Salvador

U.S. State Department

The following viewpoint is excerpted from a special report on Communist involvement in El Salvador published by the U.S. State Department. The report, with additional background information on El Salvador compiled by the State Department, can be found in the March 1981 issue of the *Department of State Bulletin.*

Consider the following questions while reading:

1. In the State Department's opinion, what is the cause of the current unrest in El Salvador?
2. How does the State Department describe the present government?
3. What conclusions does the State Department arrive at?

U.S. State Department, "Communist Interference in El Salvador," *Department of State Bulletin,* March, 1981.

This special report presents definitive evidence of the clandestine military support given by the Soviet Union, Cuba, and their Communist allies to Marxist-Leninist guerrillas now fighting to overthrow the established Government of El Salvador. The evidence, drawn from captured guerrilla documents and war materiel and corroborated by intelligence reports, underscores the central role played by Cuba and other Communist countries beginning in 1979 in the political unification, military direction, and arming of insurgent forces in El Salvador...

ARMS FLOW INTO EL SALVADOR

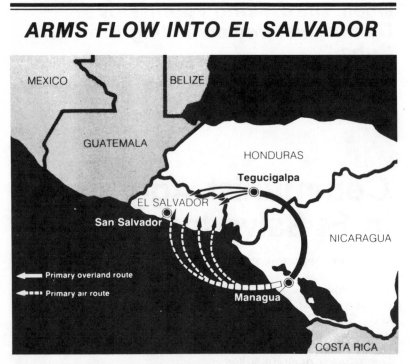

"In December, Salvadoran guerrillas, encouraged by Cuba, begin plans for a general offensive in early 1981. To provide the increased support necessary, the Sandinistas revive the airlift into El Salvador...Overland arms shipments also continue through Honduras from Nicaragua and Costa Rica."

From Special Report #80, "Communist Interference in El Salvador," the United States Department of State, February 23, 1981.

It is clear that over the past year the insurgency in El Salvador has been progressively transformed into another case of indirect armed aggression against a small Third World country by Communist powers acting through Cuba.

The United States considers it of great importance that the American people and the world community be aware of the gravity of the actions of Cuba, the Soviet Union, and other Communist states who are carrying out what is clearly shown to be a well-coordinated, covert effort to bring about the overthrow of El Salvador's established government and to impose in its place a Communist regime with no popular support.

A CASE OF COMMUNIST MILITARY INVOLVEMENT IN THE THIRD WORLD

The situation in El Salvador presents a strikingly familiar case of Soviet, Cuban, and other Communist military involvement in a politically troubled Third World country. By providing arms, training, and direction to a local insurgency and by supporting it with a global propaganda campaign, the Communists have intensified and widened the conflict, greatly increased the suffering of the Salvadoran people, and deceived much of the world about the true nature of the revolution. Their objective in El Salvador as elsewhere is to bring about — at little cost to themselves — the overthrow of the established government and the imposition of a Communist regime in defiance of the will of the Salvadoran people.

El Salvador's extreme left, which includes the long-established Communist Party of El Salvador (PCES) and several armed groups of more recent origin, has become increasingly committed since 1976 to a military solution. A campaign of terrorism — bombings, assassinations, kidnappings, and seizures of embassies — has disrupted national life and claimed the lives of many innocent people.

During 1980, previously fragmented factions of the extreme left agreed to coordinate their actions in support of a joint military battle plan developed with Cuban assistance. As a precondition for large-scale Cuban aid, Salvadoran guerrilla leaders, meeting in Havana in May, formed first the Unified Revolutionary Directorate (DRU) as their central executive arm for political and military planning and, in late 1980, the Farabundo Marti People's Liberation Front (FMLN), as the coordinating body of the guerrilla organizations. A front organization, the Revolutionary Democratic Front (FDR), was also created to disseminate propaganda abroad. For appearances sake, three small non-Marxist-Leninist political parties were brought into the front, though they have no representation in the DRU.

The Salvadoran guerrillas, speaking through the FDR, have managed to deceive many about what is happening in El Salvador. They have been aided by Nicaragua and by the worldwide propaganda networks of Cuba, the Soviet Union, and other Communist countries.

U.S. MUST SUPPORT EL SALVADOR

The United States cannot stand idly by while a reformist government comes under attack by externally advised and armed guerrilla groups that lack popular support. If we fail to make clear that the external encouragement of violence and instability in El Salvador will have serious costs, we insure that other countries seeking domestic solutions to domestic problems will find their efforts thwarted by guerrilla groups advised and armed from abroad. In turn, our failure to respond adequately to externally supported attempts to overthrow governments committed to reforms and to electoral solutions would cause other friendly countries to doubt our ability to help them resist assaults on their sovereignty.

Current Policy #265, U.S. Department of State, March 19, 1981.

The guerrillas' propaganda aims at legitimizing their violence and concealing the Communist aid that makes it possible. Other key aims are to discredit the Salvadoran Government, to misrepresent U.S. policies and actions, and to foster the impression of overwhelming popular support for the revolutionary movement...

In addition to media propaganda, Cuba and the Soviet Union promote the insurgent cause at international forums, with individual governments, and among foreign opinion leaders. Cuba has an efficient network for introducing and promoting representatives of the Salvadoran left all over the world. Havana and Moscow also bring indirect pressure on some governments to support the Salvadoran revolutionaries by mobilizing local Communist groups.

COMMUNIST MILITARY INTERVENTION:
A CHRONOLOGY

Before September 1980 the diverse guerrilla groups in El Salvador were ill-coordinated and ill-equipped, armed with pistols and a varied assortment of hunting rifles and shotguns. At that time the insurgents acquired weapons predominantly through purchases on the international market and from dealers who participated in the supply of arms to the Sandinistas in Nicaragua.

By January 1981 when the guerrillas launched their "general offensive," they had acquired an impressive array of modern weapons and supporting equipment never before used in El Salvador by either the insurgents or the military...

Recently acquired evidence has enabled us to reconstruct the central role played by Cuba, other Communist countries, and several radical states in the political unification and military direction of insurgent forces in El Salvador and in equipping them in less than 6 months with a panoply of modern weapons that enabled the guerrillas to launch a well-armed offensive.

This information, which we consider incontrovertible, has been acquired over the past year...

THE GOVERNMENT:
THE SEARCH FOR ORDER AND DEMOCRACY

Central America's smallest and most densely populated country is El Salvador. Since its independence in 1821, the country has experienced chronic political instability and repression, widespread poverty, and concentration of wealth and power in the hands of a few families. Although considerable economic progress took place in the 1960s, the political system remained in the hands of a traditional economic elite backed by the military. During the 1970s, both the legitimate grievances of the poor and landless and the growing aspirations of the expanding middle classes met increasingly with repression. El Salvador has long been a violent country with political, economic, and personal disputes often resulting in murder.

133

Aware of the need for change and alarmed by the prospect of Nicaragua-like chaos, progressive Salvadoran military officers and civilians overthrew the authoritarian regime of General Carlos Humberto Romero in October 1979 and ousted nearly 100 conservative senior officers.

After an initial period of instability, the new government stabilized around a coalition that includes military participants in the October 1979 coup, the Christian Democratic Party, and independent civilians. Since March 1980, this coalition has begun broad social changes: conversion of large estates into peasant cooperatives, distribution of land to tenant farmers, and nationalization of foreign trade and banking.

Four Marxist-Leninist guerrilla groups are using violence and terrorism against the Salvadoran Government and its reforms. Three small non-Marxist-Leninist political parties — including a Social Democratic Party — work with guerrilla organizations and their political fronts through the Democratic Revolutionary Front (FDR), most of whose activities take place outside El Salvador.

The Government of El Salvador — headed since last December by Jose Napoleon Duarte, the respected Christian Democrat denied office by the military in the Presidential elections of 1972 — faces armed opposition from the extreme right as well as from the left. Exploiting their traditional ties to the security forces and the tendency of some members of the security forces to abuse their authority, some wealthy Salvadorans affected by the Duarte government's reforms have sponsored terrorist activities against supporters of the agrarian and banking reforms and against the government itself...

Despite bitter resistance from right and left, the Duarte government has stuck to its reform programs and has adopted emergency measures to ease the lot of the poor through public works, housing projects, and aid to marginal communities. On the political front, it has offered amnesty to its opponents, scheduled elections for a constituent assembly in 1982, and pledged to hand power over to a popularly elected government no later than mid-1983.

The government's pursuit of progress with order has been further hampered by the virtual breakdown of the law enforcement and judicial system and by the lack of an effective civil service.

'DON'T MOVE — IT COULD BE ANOTHER VIETNAM'

THE VIETNAM SYNDROME

EL SALVADOR

The introduction of the reforms — some of which are now clearly irreversible — has reduced popular support for those who argue that change can only come about through violence.

Few Salvadorans participate in antigovernment demonstrations. Repeated calls by the guerrillas for general strikes in mid-and late 1980 went unheeded. The Duarte government, moreover, has made clear its willingness to negotiate the terms of future political processes with democratic members of all opposition forces — most notably, by accepting the offer of El Salvador's Council of Bishops to mediate between the government and the Democratic Revolutionary Front.

In sum, the Duarte government is working hard and with some success to deal with the serious political, social, and economic problems that most concern the people of El Salvador.

U.S. SUPPORT

In its commitment to reform and democracy, the Government of El Salvador has had the political support of the United States ever since the October 1979 revolution. Because we give primary emphasis to helping the people of El Salvador, most of our assistance has been economic. In 1980, the United States provided nearly $56 million in aid, aimed at easing the conditions that underlie unrest and extremism. This assistance has helped create jobs, feed the hungry, improve health and housing and education, and support the reforms that are opening and modernizing El Salvador's economy. The United States will continue to work with the Salvadoran Government toward economic betterment, social justice, and peace.

Because the solution in El Salvador should be of the Salvadorans' own making and nonviolent, the United States has carefully limited its military support. In January, mounting evidence of Communist involvement compelled President Carter to authorize a resupply of weapons and ammunition to El Salvador — the first provision of lethal items since 1977.

SOME CONCLUSIONS

The foregoing record leaves little doubt that the Salvadoran insurgency has become the object of a large-scale commitment by Communist states outside Latin America.

1. The political direction, organization, and arming of the insurgency is coordinated and heavily influenced by Cuba — with active support of the Soviet Union, East Germany, Vietnam, and other Communist states.
2. The massing and delivery of arms to the Salvadoran guerrillas by those states must be judged against the fact that from

1977 until January 1981 the United States provided no weapons or ammunition to the Salvadoran Armed Forces.

3. A major effort has been made to provide "cover" for this operation by supplying arms of Western manufacture and by supporting a front organization known as the Democratic Revolutionary Front to seek non-Communist political support through propaganda.

4. Although some non-Communist states have also provided material support, the organization and delivery of this assistance, like the overwhelming mass of arms, are in the hands of Communist-controlled networks.

In short, over the past year, the insurgency in El Salvador has been progressively transformed into a textbook case of indirect armed aggression by Communist powers through Cuba.

"The U.S. should change its course to avert further disaster, both for Salvadorans and for the United States."

The U.S. Should Change Its Salvadoran Policy

Phillip Berryman

The following viewpoint is excerpted from a statement made before the Subcommittee on Inter-American Affairs of the House Foreign Relations Committee on March 11, 1981. Mr. Berryman made the remarks on behalf of the American Friends Service Committee. The AFSC is a Quaker organization supported by individuals of different faiths who care about social justice and humanitarian service. From 1976 until the present Mr. Berryman has been AFSC Central America representative. He now serves in the AFSC Peace Education Program.

Consider the following questions while reading:

1. From what experience does Mr. Berryman express his viewpoint?
2. What is the author's response to the State Department "White Paper" concerning El Salvador, dated February 23, 1981?
3. How does the author react to the State Department claim that outside forces are trying to impose a communist government against the will of the Salvadoran people?

This viewpoint is reprinted with permission from the American Friends Service Comittee.

From 1965 to 1973 I worked in a Panama City barrio with the Catholic Church. From May 1976 until the present I have been AFSC Central America representative with a primary responsibility to interpret events in the region for people in the United States. Until July, 1980, I lived in Guatemala and traveled extensively in Central America. Since that time I have been doing public education on Central America in the U.S. My most recent trip to Central America was in November of last year.

In El Salvador AFSC has maintained wide contacts and has tried to see the situation through the eyes of the poor, and those people working with them, largely Church people. I have been in contact with academics and moderate politicians, labor and peasant leaders...

In introduction I assert that what one sees in El Salvador depends very much on the angle of vision and what one is looking for. Most particularly, I think there is a great temptation for policy makers to overlook the great majority of the people of a country like El Salvador and to focus just on elites, whether it be ruling elites or what are assumed to be small groups of revolutionaries...

All along, U.S. policy seems to have been based on the assumption that the majority of people are not genuinely involved. It is sometimes said they simply want to be left in peace.

In other words, the bulk of the Salvadoran people are apparently left out of the equation as formulated by the U.S....

WHAT IS HAPPENING IN EL SALVADOR?

The most recent comprehensive statement of the U.S. government's analysis of the situation in El Salvador is contained in the State Department "White Paper" of February 23, 1981. The central part of this document is a chronology of alleged contacts between Salvadoran revolutionaries and communist and radical organizations or governments. The paper seeks to prove that the insurgency in El Salvador has been transformed into an instance of an outside power attempting to impose a communist government against the will of the Salvadoran people...

In commenting on the White Paper, I hope to make clear that the erroneous political analysis in that document constitutes a dangerous foundation for U.S. policy in El Salvador.

1. The White Paper *lacks a historical sense* of how the present situation arose. Aside from a sentence about people's aspirations being met with repression during the 1970s, there is no mention of the whole series of events which led to the present crisis. All the stress is on communist interference starting in 1979.

A few examples of omitted recent historical factors are grass-roots organizing by the Catholic Church going back a decade, the development of popular organizations, the electoral frauds of 1972 and 1977, the proposed land reform in 1976 that was halted by the Salvadoran oligarchy, and the increasing repression of church people and popular leaders. In sum, there is no apparent consideration of Salvadoran history by U.S. policy-makers.

2. The document persists in calling the present Salvadoran government one which has effected *broad social changes* and which faces *armed opposition from the extreme right and the extreme left.*

Quite frankly, few persons in Central America believe that, though that is what readers of the U.S. press see. It is certainly

Don Wright, *The Miami News.*

not the perception in El Salvador, nor in Mexico or Europe where press coverage has been more sophisticated...

3. It is *asserted that there is an international communist campaign* to discredit the Salvadoran government. The document makes no mention of *Amnesty International,* no mention of a number of reputable organizations which have gone to El Salvador during the last year and a half, such as church delegations and a group examining medical abuses; no mention was made of the visit of U.S. Representatives Mikulski, Studds and Edgar.

Most importantly, it ignores the Catholic Church's legal aid office, Socorro Juridico, and the Salvadoran Human Rights Commission. These latter have documented case by case the repression against the people in documents which the committee undoubtedly has at its disposal.

The Catholic Church is in a position to have direct information, particularly in the countryside. It has repeatedly stated that the great majority of the victims of violence are unarmed civilians killed by official forces or officially tolerated right wing bands.

Thus it is grossly misleading to attribute the international image of the Salvadoran government to a communist campaign.

4. *The much touted land reform has largely turned out to be a pretext for and a means to military control of the countryside.*

It benefits relatively few peasants and does nothing for those without lands who make up 40% of the peasantry. The coffee oligarchy lands are virtually untouched.

There are numerous well-documented cases of the land reform being used to eliminate peasant leadership. Shortly after the reform was decreed, I talked to a refugee who was not part of the opposition, whom troops had imprisoned, tortured for several days, and shot in the head, leaving him, they thought, for dead.

5. The document gives a *mistaken view of the left opposition.* In the first place, it *exaggerates the importance of the Salvadoran Communist Party (SCP)...*

6. There is no mention in the State Department White Paper of the "popular" organizations, large mass groups which are the

most significant political force in El Salvador. On January 22, 1980 they held a demonstration in which 200,000 people marched: 4% of the population of the country. To demonstrate is to risk being attacked and this demonstration was attacked by snipers.

NEGATIVE VIEW OF U.S. POLICY

The United States Government, above all, cannot "solve" anything here. Since it has, for the moment, chosen to speak the language of war, it can at best raise the number of casualties one side inflicts on the other and on the scores of defenseless civilians in between — who, make no bones about it, numerically suffer more casualties at the hands of the Government forces than at those of the guerrillas. This is perfectly understood everywhere from the sorriest slum of Mejicanos to the deepest bowels of the State Department.

U.S. policy has not explored peace; it has shunted aside all talk of mediation and negotiation with bravado and bluster. It is reaping increasingly negative international responses with this position, from old allies in Europe and new clients in the Third World, who see their own good-faith offers blunted by the U.S. stance and who express horror at the consequences and scorn at the hypocrisy of its policies.

Anne Nelson, *Christianity and Crisis*, July 20, 1981.

7. The document treats the FDR (Democratic Revolutionary Front) as simply a front for the guerrillas and only mentions "three small political parties" as belonging. It *neglects to mention the popular organizations* (which include the bulk of the country's unions), the universities, a bus owners organization, a small business organization, an organization of professionals, among others.

The document says most of the FDR's activities take place outside El Salvador. I find this statement incredible since I talked in San Salvador to Enrique Alvarez Córdoba, the president of the FDR and two other top leaders, just days before they and others were picked up, tortured and killed, in what was clearly an action of government forces, despite official denials.

8. It is repeatedly stated that the opposition has little popular support. The "failed" January offensive is cited as proof. But, if the opposition had little support, why rush many millions of dollars, as well as much equipment, and advisors?...

Certainly the question of popular support is the key one. The extent of the opposition's support remains to be seen, although my research leads me to conclude that it is considerable. What is beyond question to me is that the junta government has no popular support. The Christian Democratic party scarcely exists except in the leaders who are working for the government.

9. Cuba is presented as the unifier and organizer of the Salvadoran insurgency. It is accurate that the revolutionaries have over the years visited Cuba, received training there; undoubtedly there are close contacts. But it does not necessarily follow that such contacts prove that Fidel Castro or the Cuban government is orchestrating the Salvadoran opposition.

Put briefly: The State Department White Paper pictures the situation as follows: a small group of Communists, coordinated and supplied from Cuba (and ultimately the Soviet Union) using a non-representative Front, are seeking to overthrow the legitimate Salvadoran government which is seeking to make needed reforms, while withstanding pressure from right and left.

My impression is entirely different: there is a large popular insurgency in El Salvador, coordinated by a coalition of Marxists (mainly independent, but including the Communist Party) and non-Marxists, and it is attempting to overthrow a brutally repressive government...

WHAT CAN THE U.S. DO? — ALTERNATIVES

AFSC and the FCNL believe that the U.S. should change its course to avert further disaster, both for Salvadorans and for the United States.

Some underlying principles we suggest for U.S. policy are:

A. The starting point of any U.S. policy toward El Salvador has to be with the Salvadoran people, including the poor majority

Philip Berryman

who are peasants, very often landless. They must not be sacrificed because of some geopolitical concern or the desire to show U.S. determination to assert its power.
B. El Salvador should be viewed in terms of its own history and its own internal dynamics, and not primarily as a "case" of communist expansion.
C. The U.S. must recognize that the main problem is political — how to arrive at a stable government which represents the people and works with them toward their own development. This cannot be achieved through military means.

From these principles we make the following recommendations for U.S. conduct:

1. Other countries should be consulted and their viewpoints sought. Mexico has an even greater stake in a stable Central America than the U.S. and Mexico disagrees sharply with present U.S. policy.

2. The U.S. should recognize that the FDR is a legitimate political force and represents a real alternative for El Salvador. The U.S. should enter into serious, respectful contacts with the FDR. The U.S. should further recognize that the FDR is a genuine pluralistic coalition and that it has good reason to want good relations with the U.S. should it come to power.

3. The U.S. should end *all* military aid to El Salvador.

4. The U.S. should encourage efforts to find a negotiated solution to the crisis in El Salvador. It is unlikely the United States itself can play an active role in negotiations since by its support to the junta it has become identified with a single party in the dispute.

"Our actions with regard to El Salvador have as their goal the reduction of violence and instability in order to facilitate a peaceful transition to an elected government."

U.S. Involvement Promotes Peace and Stability

Walter J. Stoessel, Jr.

Walter J. Stoessel, Jr. is currently Under Secretary of State for Political Affairs. He served as Ambassador to Poland from 1968 to 1972 and Ambassador to the Federal Republic of Germany from 1976 to 1981. Mr. Stoessel has been with the U.S. Foreign Service since 1942, shortly after his graduation from Stanford University. In the following viewpoint, he explains the reasons for U.S. support and aid to the Duarte government of El Salvador.

Consider the following questions while reading:
1. Who does the U.S. government support in the El Salvadoran struggle, and for what reason?
2. What kind of aid is the U.S. giving the El Salvadoran government?
3. What three alternatives does the author claim exist in El Salvador?

Walter J. Stoessel, Jr., "Review of El Salvador," *Department of State Bulletin*, April, 1981.

Our actions with regard to El Salvador have as their goal the reduction of violence and instability in order to facilitate a peaceful transition to an elected government. This is the goal of the Salvadoran people and of their current government, headed by Christian Democratic President Jose Napoleon Duarte, which we strongly support. Having already promulgated a far-reaching agrarian reform and changes in the banking system and export trade, the government last week moved the country closer to elections when President Duarte appointed an electoral commission.

These important reforms will contribute to the reduction of violence and political instability in the longer term. In the short term, however, some landowners availed themselves of tradi-

Walter J. Stoessel, Jr.

tional ties to local security forces, while Cuban-supported guerrillas attempted to exploit popular resentment of past authorities. Both these extremes sought to undermine the reforms through violence but for different reasons. The landowners wished to restore the status quo ante; the guerrillas saw that reforms were winning away their popular support and recruitment base.

In recent months, our understanding of the situation in El Salvador has changed with the discovery that large quantities of arms and munitions were being supplied to the guerrillas. Last summer and fall, far away Vietnam, Ethiopia, and some Eastern European countries joined Cuba to take the initiative to transform an essentially domestic conflict in Central America into an international confrontation. These outside efforts to impose an unpopular military solution proved unacceptable to the Salvadoran people, who rejected the guerrillas' appeals for support. The Carter Administration acted once it acquired the evidence. We have done likewise.

The United States cannot stand idly by while a reformist government comes under attack by externally advised and armed guerrilla groups that lack popular support. If we fail to make clear that the external encouragement of violence and instability in El Salvador will have serious costs, we insure that other countries seeking domestic solutions to domestic problems will find their efforts thwarted by guerrilla groups advised and armed from abroad. In turn, our failure to respond adequately to externally supported attempts to overthrow governments committed to reforms and to electoral solutions would cause other friendly countries to doubt our ability to help them resist assaults on their sovereignty.

ECONOMIC AID

While the guerrillas in El Salvador are externally supported, they also feed on domestic ills. These include years of repressive and unresponsive governments and inequitable distribution of resources and life opportunities. For this reason, the major emphasis of our assistance program for El Salvador is economic rather than military. The Government of El Salvador welcomes this emphasis. Since October 1979, Salvadoran authorities have been committed to leading their country to democracy. To that end, the Duarte government is today working to carry out basic economic reforms.

We strongly support these efforts, financially as well as morally...

Our aid is designed to help the Duarte government eradicate the chronic social and economic ills that have fostered unrest. El Salvador's needs are enormous and pressing. We hope that our allies and other friendly countries — many of which have themselves urged that socioeconomic needs not be neglected —will go beyond exhortations and join us in providing economic assistance to El Salvador. The general climate of violence and the guerrillas' purposeful destruction of foodstuffs, electrical installations, communications lines, vehicles, and roads have cut deeply into El Salvador's production and growth. The suffering of the Salvadoran people in this chaotic situation requires a compassionate response from us and from all civilized nations.

SECURITY ASSISTANCE

Now let me address our security assistance efforts. We are providing the necessary military assistance to the Duarte government in its battle against the externally supported guerrillas. Let me assure you that we are doing this with the greatest

---

DEMOCRATIC SOCIETIES ARE UNDER ASSAULT

If present trends are not arrested, the convergence of rising international disorder, greater Western vulnerability, and growing Soviet military power will undo the international codes of conduct that foster the peaceful resolution of disputes between nations. The symptoms of this breakdown — terrorism, subversion, and conquest — are already apparent. The ideals and safety of democratic societies are under assault.

Secretary of State Alexander Haig, 1981.

---

prudence and caution and with the lessons of the past very much in mind. El Salvador is not another Vietnam. Our objectives are limited: to help the government with its problems of training, equipment repair and maintenance, mobility, and re-supply...

A TASTE OF HONEY...

BOB DIX—
UNION
LEADER

Reprinted by permission from the *Manchester Union Leader*.

COMMITMENT TO A PEACEFUL OUTCOME

Our economic and military assistance are both important for an eventual political resolution of the conflict in El Salvador. A peaceful outcome will require both greater social justice and greater stability under the law...

We also suport President Duarte's offers to discuss with opposition leaders and with business, labor, and church groups within El Salvador what structures and guarantees will best insure open elections next year. We cannot, of course, participate directly in any negotiation process that would compromise the sovereignty of El Salvador and the right of its government to negotiate on its own behalf. We are strongly committed, however, to a peaceful transition to an elected government and oppose any and all attempts to deprive the Salvadoran people of their right to elect a government of their choosing. We firmly oppose any kind of coup against the centrist government.

In our view, the Duarte government provides the best opportunity for a transition to a political system that will offer the Salvadoran people some measure of control over the decisions that affect their lives. We support it for that reason. In El Salvador, as in any country, we have to deal with the political possibilities as they exist now. There are three alternatives in El Salvador today — the forces of the extreme right, the forces of the extreme left, and the present government. Of these, the Duarte government is the only one that promises to lead a transition to full constitutional order.

Should it come to power, the extreme left would probably create a government modeled, like Cuba's, on that of the Soviet Union. Such governments can vary among themselves, but we do know from history that they have an unusual ability to establish a rigid grip. To passively accept a Cuban-coordinated attempt to impose their kind of political order by force of arms would be to close off all but one narrow path for the future development of the Salvadoran people. This is what we want to help prevent.

In summary, we believe the measured steps we have taken and have proposed are reasonable and responsible. They are carefully designed to contribute to a lessening of the violence and instability that threaten the social and political reforms the Duarte government has courageously undertaken. I hope that we will have the support of the Congress, and of this committee, as we proceed to develop U.S. policy toward El Salvador and the region.

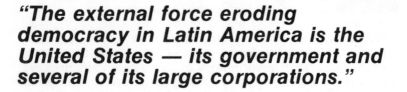

VIEWPOINT 6

"The external force eroding democracy in Latin America is the United States — its government and several of its large corporations."

U.S. Involvement Promotes Repression

Eldon Kenworthy

A PhD in political science from Yale, Eldon Kenworthy is Professor of Latin American Politics and U.S.-Latin American Relations at Cornell University. In the July, 1981, issue of *Democracy,* Professor Kenworthy examines the tactics which the U.S. government has used to justify support of a "military rightest regime" in El Salvador. In the following viewpoint, he concludes that the "external force" eroding democracy in Latin America is not the communists, but the United States.

Consider the following questions while reading:

1. How does the author relate the lessening of democracy with U.S. Empire?
2. In the author's opinion, what three tactics does the U.S. use to preserve its empire in Latin America?
3. Why does the author claim revolution rather than reform is necessary in El Salvador?
4. What does the author think the U.S. should do in El Salvador?

Eldon Kenworthy, "The U.S. and Latin America: Empire vs. Social Change," *Democracy,* July, 1981. Copyright 1981 by the Common Good Foundation.

The Reagan administration's policy on El Salvador is clear. "The insurgency in El Salvador," the State Department has stated, is "a textbook case of indirect armed aggression by Communist powers"...

One of the lessons Washington draws from Vietnam is that sustained intervention abroad, in proxy situations where the "true" adversary is masked, may not be "understood" by the public. Without public understanding, youth refuse induction, Congress grows restive, presidents decline reelection, and our involvement consequently winds down, damaging credibility. To portray the Salvadoran opposition as homogeneously communist, externally supported, and linked to our major adversary leaves nothing to chance. No complex explanations to befuddle the public's mind. In congressional testimony in February, the Acting Assistant Secretary of State for Inter-American Affairs, John Bushell, repeatedly referred to "the other side" and "the worldwide Communist network" in discussing El Salvador. What could be simpler?

U.S. EMPIRE AND DEMOCRACY

There is a problem, however, that goes deeper than this difficulty in leading the public through a maze of proxydom and anticipated damage to credibility. It is the dilemma long faced by Britain and now confronting the United States: how to reconcile democracy at home with empire abroad. Concretely, the "friendly" Third World governments that most consistently support Washington are, with notable exceptions, among the world's more repressive regimes. It's not easy to accept these governments as fellow members of the "free-world." South Africa free? South Korea? Pakistan? Pinochet's Chile? It's harder still to convince taxpayers and parents to expend money and blood to maintain these regimes in power. In the great geopolitical game the rulers of Argentina, the Phillipines, Indonesia, and Guatemala bat on our side, albeit low in the order. At home where they have real power, these rulers contradict the very values on which our claim to world leadership is based. That's the contradiction of empire and democracy.

THREE TACTICS TO PRESERVE THE EMPIRE

More than most presidents, Carter admitted the dilemma. His human rights policy drew a distinction between friendly governments that shared our basic values and those that didn't. A price had to be paid for this distinction: the alienation of some friendly governments, and the administration's own inconsistency when it came to countries too strategic to offend. Reagan and Haig have reverted to three older ways of trying to reconcile the democracy-empire dilemma. These three tactics, I would suggest, take us a long way toward understanding Washington's distorted presentation of the Salvadoran situation.

One element in this presentation, we have seen, is the renaming of the drama: what is internal becomes international. If we are being tested by "the other side," our very survival is at stake. Under such circumstances, who would question the credentials of an ally? A second tactic is to recast the players, not only turning the rebels into foreigners but turning the rightists into reformers. If our "friends" are reformers, the contradiction between empire and democracy evaporates...

The result is what we see in El Salvador today: a rightist regime, its power lodged in the military, with a facade of civilian reform Washington can use to satisfy domestic and international public opinion...

Here, however, I take up the third and final way of trying to escape the empire-democracy contradiction: replacing present with future.

Should the Left triumph in El Salvador, Henry Kissinger asserted in a speech delivered March 9, 1981, there will be "infinitely more suffering" than if "the alternative" prevails. Autocracies, Jeane Kirkpatrick lectures us, may evolve into democracies, whereas totalitarianism is irreversible. Almost by definition in Kirkpatrick's scheme, only Marxism degenerates into totalitarianism (so quickly is fascism forgotten). This tactic permits Washington to identify with the people of a Latin American country, claiming to act in their best interests even if they are not cognizant of it. So when the U.S. Senate published irrefutable evidence of high-level Washington involvement in destabilizing the democratically elected government of Salvador Allende, President Ford simply said we acted "in the best interests of the people of Chile."

The obvious advantage of this tactic is that it is irrefutable. A prediction about the future cannot be disproved in the present...

These three solutions to the empire-democracy dilemma share one requirement: ignorance. They work to the extent that the U.S. public knows little about Latin America. Perhaps this explains why nearly every incoming administration finds it hard to appoint an Assistant Secretary of State for this region and why the person eventually chosen invariably is unknown to the community of scholars specializing in Latin America...

REVOLUTION INSTEAD OF REFORM

What obvious truths about Latin America must be suppressed for U.S. policy to make sense to its citizens? Returning to the central question — Why revolution? — the first obvious truth is that armed insurrection has long been part of the Latin American political process. If U.S. citizens talk of "critical elections," Latin Americans speak of revolutions. In some countries practically each generation has had "its" uprising, attempted or successful. Revolutionary leaders are popular heroes (Marti, Zapata, Sandino, Guevara). Thus revolution is not, as North Americans view it, some immaculate conception that launches a nation, thereafter to be revisited only in ritual.

DOES THE END JUSTIFY THE MEANS?

The Reagan Administration — and, to be fair, the Carter Administration before it — has chosen to pin halo and wings on Jose Napoleon Duarte and surround him with a choir of frightened Christian Democrat acolytes. To whatever extent he is lacking in the role, there is a compensating crowd of pure devils, played by an "extreme left," which threatens to turn the country into a toy Gulag and swarm up into Texas besides. The answer is, as ever, in our hands: to arm the angels. And if their spear-carriers turn out to bear a striking resemblance to ugly and repressive military dictators we've known in the past, then one must realize that the end, which is democracy, justifies the means, which is killing "subversives."

Anne Nelson, *Christianity and Crisis*, July 20, 1981.

Equally indigenous to the region are Marxist movements, which formed in most countries more than half a century ago. Avowed communists have served in governments, led unions, taught in universities, won Nobel prizes. There have been good Marxists and bad — though fewer corrupt ones than is the norm in other political parties. The point is: Marxism has become as indigenous to the region as the revolutionary and nationalist traditions to which it frequently is joined.

But why do Latin Americans turn to revolution — and sometimes to Marxism — rather than to less costly forms of political change? the answer is simple: the other forms frequently don't work...

A large part of the explanation, however, rests with El Salvador's experience with reform. Salvadorans have seen reforms announced and aborted many times. Civilian reformers never got beyond the ballot box...

Reform works when elites are willing to make concessions. Elites resist concessions when the gap between them and the masses is as vast as it is in El Salvador. If democracy were deeply institutionalized, giving the many leverage with the wealthy, concessions might still occur. What North Americans forget is that elections are not binding in Latin America. They are reversed by military coup so regularly that the mere threat of a coup (known as *planteo)* is sufficient to deter most civilian reformers. All an elite needs to perpetuate its privileged position, then, is an alliance with key officers. In a country such as El Salvador a symbiotic relationship develops, military officers being cut into business and prestige while the "Fourteen Families" (the economic elite) are granted immunity from reform.

THE ANTICOMMUNISM LABEL

The ideology that glues this alliance together and also, if played right, that commits Washington to pick up the tab, is anticommunism. Thus any challenge to the status quo is labeled communist, even if carried out by Catholic clergy. To the Latin American military mind an opponent is an enemy and an enemy is to be killed. The free use of the communist label in such polarized situations as El Salvador contributes to the free use of assassination.

North Americans too fear communism and are prone to talk about it as an ominous force in the world. For most U.S. citizens, however, this remains abstract, distant. Should they meet a visiting Russian or Chinese, they are courteous; most do not advocate a preemptive strike to rid the world of communist power. Received in El Salvador, Chile, or other parts of Latin America, however, this highly symbolic anticommunism becomes deadly real. It leads to the slaughter of "sympathizers," including those who merely call for human rights. More than one U.S. congressman has returned from Latin America stunned to discover that the right wing there is not our wing. Having dealt with the Salvadoran military at close range for some time, ex-Ambassador White doesn't mince words:

> To the extent that you emphasize a military solution in El Salvador, you are going to be buttressing one of the most out-of-control, violent, bloodthirsty groups of men in the world. They have killed — at a minimum — 5,000 or 6,000 kids, just on the mere suspicion that they were involved with the leftists.

ECONOMIC REFORM

Couldn't reform come from the private sector, even though the political channel is blocked?...

Here again, a theory with some grounding in U.S. historical experience does not find an echo in Latin American reality, the key difference being Latin America's turning outward for markets and technologies. This outward orientation has gen-

Reprinted by permission from the *Minnesota Daily.*

erated economies that provide the opportunities desired by the middle and upper classes. It contains, however, no incentive for income redistribution, for labor absorption, or for production geared to the needs of the poorest half of the population.

Where oriented outward, capitalism fails that portion of the population that doesn't have the price of admission to the market. With unemployment caused by capital-intensive technologies introduced by the multinationals, and without the welfare systems found in postindustrial societies, poor people cannot buy what they need. Few of their skills are marketable in the new industries, while the land on which they might grow food has been taken for large-scale export crops...

As of 1975, four-fifths of the Salvadoran population earned less than the $704 estimated to be the minimum a family of six (the average size) needs to survive for a year. Two percent of the population, at the other pole, received roughly half the national income. It is hard to believe that the private sector can remedy this inequity...

THE U.S. IS THE ENEMY

From this perspective, it is apparent that the external force eroding democracy in Latin America is the United States — its government and several of its large corporations. No wonder, then, that Washington's rhetoric must scramble the picture, recasting the parts and substituting hypothetical futures for the palpable present.

So when President Reagan escalates military aid to the Salvadoran junta...he is signaling a commitment to support the Salvadoran right on its terms. By refusing to let his subordinates confer with representatives of the left, Reagan signals the junta that it too need not negotiate a way out of this bloodbath. Introducing Huey helicopters and Green Beret advisers is, again, an escalation that tells the Salvadoran hardliners they need not seek any but a military solution. Against this, the automatic weapons and mortars the guerrillas receive from abroad (purchased from U.S. mafiosos operating through Panama as well as donated by Vietnam, Ethiopia, Bulgaria, etc.) are no match.

The United States need not take sides in Latin American civil wars. All we need do, to paraphrase a Reagan campaign slogan, is get our government off their backs.

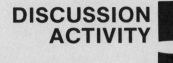
EVALUATING SOURCES OF INFORMATION

For every controversial issue there are many spokespersons who have opposing viewpoints. Each claims that his or her solution is best. In deciding how to deal with the issue, it is difficult for the average person to determine which spokesperson or expert is correct. In determining one's stance on an issue, the critical stage becomes that of deciding which source of information is most reliable.

This discussion activity should give you practice in *evaluating sources of information,* which is the ability to choose from among several alternative sources those which are the most reliable and accurate in relation to a given subject.

INSTRUCTIONS

PART I

Working in groups of four to six students, each group should rank the experts or sources on the following page. Assign the number *1* to the source you feel would give the most reliable answer to the question *"How Should the U.S. Deal With The Situation In El Salvador?"* Assign the number *2* to the second most reliable source, and so on, until all the sources have been ranked.

PART II

Each group should compare and defend its ranking with others in the class in a classwide discussion.

How Should the U.S. Deal With The Situation In El Salvador?

_____ 1. Alexander Solzhenitsyn

_____ 2. U.S. State Department

_____ 3. A representative of Amnesty International

_____ 4. A U.S. journalist assigned to Latin America

_____ 5. A German journalist assigned to Latin America

_____ 6. Phillip Berryman (the author of viewpoint 4)

_____ 7. Walter J. Stoessel (the author of viewpoint 5)

_____ 8. The president of El Salvador

_____ 9. President Ronald Reagan

_____ 10. The Russian ambassador to El Salvador

_____ 11. The U.S. ambassador to El Salvador

_____ 12. The Catholic Bishop of San Salvador

_____ 13. A university professor of Latin American Studies

_____ 14. A representative of the Washington Office on Latin America (see appendix)

_____ 15. A representative of the Christian Anti-Communism Crusade (see appendix)

BIBLIOGRAPHY

The following list of periodical articles deals with the subject matter of this chapter.

America • *Realpolitik in El Salvador,* March 14, 1981, p. 192.

Douglas J. Bennet, Jr. *U.S. Opportunities in a Fast Changing Third World,* **USA Today,** January, 1981, p. 19.

Dollars & Sense *Trade Unions and Revolution in El Salvador,* April, 1981, p. 6.

engage/social action forum - 56 *Third World Development: Challenge for Christians,* November, 1979, p. 4.

C. Forche *El Salvador: The Next Vietnam?,* **The Progressive,** February, 1981, p. 27.

Neal B. Freeman *The Current Wisdom: Rethinking Foreign Aid,* **National Review,** February 6, 1981, p. 81.

Mary Jane Heyl *Only One Penny for the World's Poor,* **The Christian Science Monitor,** August 25, 1980, p. 23.

Charles Krauthammer *Rich Nations, Poor Nations,* **The New Republic,** April 11, 1981, p. 20.

George Marotta *Third World: Threat or Opportunity,* **Agenda,** January/February, 1980, p. 23.

R. McGehee *C.I.A. and the White Paper on El Salvador,* **Nation,** April 11, 1981, p. 423.

Lance Morrow *The World's Double Standard,* **Time,** January 14, 1980, p. 32.

Joe Mulligan *Who Benefits? Unraveling the Strings Attached to U.S. Foreign Aid,* **Sojourners,** February, 1981, p. 10.

New Guard *Why We Must Aid El Salvador,* special section, Summer, 1981, p. 15.

The New Republic *Salvaging El Salvador,* March 21, 1981, p. 5.

Jeremiah Novak *In Defense of the Third World,* **America,** January 21, 1978, p. 34.

William D. Rogers *The Stakes in El Salvador,* **Newsweek,** March 30, 1981, p. 15.

Kenneth W. Thompson *Foreign Policy and World Poverty,* **USA Today,** November, 1980, p. 20.

R. White *El Salvador's Future — And How U.S. Can Influence It,* **U.S. News & World Report,** January 26, 1981, p. 37.

APPENDIX OF ORGANIZATIONS

The following organizations are concerned with the foreign policy issues discussed in this book.

American Foreign Policy Institute
499 South Capital Street, Suite 500
Washington, D.C. 20003
(202) 484-1676

The 36 member Institute, founded in 1968, sponsors conferences and symposia on defense related issues of foreign policy. Publications include *Conference Proceedings* and special studies.

American Jewish League Against Communism
39 East 68th Street
New York, NY 10021
(212) 472-1400

The AJLAC was founded in 1948 to educate U.S. citizens about the threat of communism. The group publishes *Jews Against Communism.*

American Security Council Education Foundation
Boston, VA 22713
(703) 825-1776

An educational group founded in 1958 to further public understanding of the "basic foundation of American strength and freedom and the Communist challenge to American freedom." Publications include the quarterly *International Security Affairs,* handbooks and studies.

Association of Third World Affairs
2011 Kalorama Road N.W.
Washington, D.C. 20009
(202) 966-9326

The association, founded in 1966, promotes cooperation between Americans and groups in developing countries. Publications include the bimonthly *Third World Forum* and occasional monographs.

Cardinal Mindszenty Foundation
P.O. Box 11321
St. Louis, MO 63105
(314) 991-2939

The Foundation, founded in 1958, conducts educational and research activities concerning communist objectives and tactics. Publications include the monthly *Mindszenty Report* and *The Red Line* plus pamphlets.

Christian Anti-Communism Crusade
P.O. Box 890
Long Beach, CA 90801
(213) 437-0941

The nonprofit educational organization, organized in 1953, is devoted to the "battle against Communism and the propagation of the Christian faith." The Crusade publishes a bimonthly newsletter available upon request. They also publish pamphlets and books and provide films, tapes and cassettes.

Coalition for a New Foreign and Military Policy
120 Maryland Avenue, N.E.
Washington, D.C. 20002
(202) 546-8400

A coalition of 40 national religious, labor, civic, peace and public interest organizations, founded in 1976, to promote the development of demilitarized, humanitarian and non-interventionist foreign policy. They provide information on foreign policy legislation and publish the monthly *Action Alerts* and the quarterly *Coalition Newsletter* and *Resource.*

Communist Party of the U.S.A.
235 West 23rd Street, Seventh floor
New York, NY 10011
(212) 989-4994

The political party of the working class, founded in 1919, has as its aim a socialist society. The party publishes the monthly *Political Affairs.*

Council on Foreign Relations
58 East 68th Street
New York, NY 10021
(212) 734-0400

Founded in 1940, the Council, formed of individuals with specialized knowledge of and interest in international affairs, studies the international aspects of American political, economic and strategic problems. Publications include the quarterly *Foreign Affairs, Annual Report* and specialized studies on various aspects of U.S. foreign policy.

Foreign Policy Association
205 Lexington Avenue
New York, NY 10016
(212) 481-8450

Founded in 1918, the FPA is a nonpartisan educational organization dedicated to stimulating interest in international relations and encouraging citizen expression of opinion on foreign policy. A free catalogue of Association publications is available from the Catalogue Department.

Foundation for Foreign Affairs
6121 North Fairfield Avenue
Chicago, IL 60659
(312) 262-4593

Founded in 1945 to promote and widen understanding of international relations, the Foundation encourages historical research and writing from differing perspectives. The Foundation publishes the *Foreign Policy Series* of books.

National Committee on American Foreign Policy, Inc.
310 Madison Avenue, Suite 1525
New York, NY 10017
(212) 697-8787

This organization of individuals, founded in 1974, attempts to stimulate informed interest and concern for the serious problems confronting the U.S. in its foreign policy. The Committee publishes a newsletter on significant world issues.

Spartacist League
P.O. Box 1377
New York, NY 10001
(212) 925-5665

The League, founded in 1966, is a "Revolutionary organization which...is committed to the task of building the party which will lead the working class to the victory of the socialist revolution in the U.S." Publications include the biweekly *Workers Vanguard*, the quarterly *Women and Revolution* as well as the "Marxist Bulletin Series" and pamphlets.

Washington Office on Latin America
110 Maryland Avenue, N.E.
Washington, DC 20002
(202) 544-8045

The WOLA was established in 1974 by a broad coalition of church persons and scholars engaged in Latin American concerns. It supports respect for basic human rights, excercise of civil liberties and democratic rule. They publish a bimonthly *Latin America Update,* available upon request, and occasional reports.

Index

MEET THE EDITOR

David L. Bender is a history graduate from the University of Minnesota. He also has a M.A. in government from St. Mary's University in San Antonio, Texas. He has taught social problems at the high school level for several years. He is the general editor of the Opposing Viewpoints Series and has authored most of the titles in the series.